Weep, Shudder, Die

ALSO BY ROBERT LEVINE

Maria Callas: A Musical Biography

The Story of the Orchestra:
Listen While You Learn About the Instruments,
the Music and the Composers Who Wrote the Music!

Weep, Shudder, Die

A GUIDE TO LOVING OPERA

Robert Levine

itbooks

AN IMPRINT OF HARPERCOLLINS PUBLISHERS

HarperCollins books may be purchased for educational, business, or sales promotional use. For information please write: Special Markets Department, HarperCollins Publishers, 10 East 53rd Street, New York, NY 10022.

FIRST EDITION

Designed by Ashley Halsey

Library of Congress Cataloging-in-Publication Data has been applied for.

ISBN 978-0-06-194131-3

11 12 13 14 15   ov/QG   10 9 8 7 6 5 4 3 2 1

Let us go singing as far as we go;
the road will be less tedious.

—Virgil, *Eclogues*

Through singing, opera must make
you weep, shudder, die.

—Vincenzo Bellini

Contents

Author's Note

It was always about loving the sound of the singing voice and wondering what it could do.

I had a nice voice as a preteen and sang "Silent Night" on the stage of P.S. 64 in the Bronx two Christmases in a row, so I knew what singing was, but let's face it, all you really need for that song is a good octave and two notes—that's why it's so popular. (The only hurdle was the leap up to the first syllable of "heav'nly"; and it still is if you start it too high.) I got a portable radio that I put under my pillow at night and played quietly: listening to the Platters sing "Only You" and "The Great Pretender" (with its alternating high A flats and B flats at the start of the reprise, which was way out of my capabilities) or the Five Satins singing "In the Still of the Night" or even Johnnie & Joe singing the wonderful "Over the Mountain, Across the Sea" was a spectacular antidote to Perry Como's eight-note range that my parents were riveted to on the television. Somehow, the wider range, both vocal and emotional—they sang high, they sang low; they whispered, they wailed—made their music more personal, more full of feeling, more exciting than Perry Como's, Vic Damone's, Eddie Fisher's, or Andy Williams's. One might think it was a black-versus-white thing at the time—what with black singers being far more exotic and therefore more interesting—but Paul Anka's "Diana" and Buddy Holly's "That'll Be the Day" were other landmarks for some reason. (Elvis Presley had, at the time, nothing to do with singing; he had to do with rebellion, James Dean, making people's parents unhappy, and being Elvis.) Later came Percy Sledge's "When a Man Loves a Woman," which begins on a high, desperate note (it's a tenor's B flat), and at about the same time, Roy Orbison appeared. He had a lowish voice, as I had by that time, and I could sing along with about three-quarters of most of his songs, in particular the amazing "Crying." But his voice had what seemed like a trick—a weird, still unbeatable upper extension: how many singers can get the high D flat (that's above high C) on the word "crying" in a perfect mixed voice (not falsetto, not chest voice)? That note sounded liked a swoon, and it almost made me faint too.

Concurrent with all of this, or even a bit earlier, was the yearly, hard-to-avoid Miss America Pageant. After the evening gown and swimsuit competitions, the gals would have to perform—the talent competition. Many tap-danced, a couple did interpretive dancing (waving their arms while holding scarves), many sang pop tunes or played piano or violin; one, I recall, showed the perfect way to pack a suitcase (this is not a joke). But at least one or two a year sang an opera aria, or part of one: "Un bel dì" from *Madama Butterfly* was a favorite; Gilda's "Caro nome" from *Rigoletto* was another. My senses were dazzled by such sounds; one aria had great drama and a big high note at the end, and the other required the singer to bounce around on tiny, bell-like tones. Was there nothing the voice could not do? At the same time, musical movies starring a man named Mario Lanza began to appear on television. Lanza was a prodigy—there's no doubt about it now; even Luciano Pavarotti, José Carreras, and Plácido Domingo cite him as an inspiration. He had begun an operatic career but was snatched up by MGM; *The Great Caruso* and *The Student Prince* were among his hits. (He does not appear in the latter, but his voice does; he walked out after a fight with the director.) He was a handsome, charismatic matinee idol (poor boy becomes a star), and he could, to my ears, express great emotion through singing with a big, dark voice; indeed, his tones seemed superhuman in a different way from Roy Orbison's. His records sold millions of copies. He was also always in the news—he drank and ate too much, rebelled against the movie studio, and was said to have Mafia connections; when he died at thirty-eight in 1959, he was probably the most famous tenor in the world. His death made big news as well: at the insistence of the studio (or the Mafia) he would periodically be admitted to a hospital and kept in a coma referred to as a "twilight sleep treatment" in order to lose weight. He died immediately after one of these sessions in Rome, of a pulmonary embolism. But I digress.

Though I paid attention to "popular music" all along, a fascination with folk music followed (Joan Baez, the Weavers, the Greenbriar Boys, Pete Seeger, et al.); it was easier to imitate and had a certain purity and "oldness" that appealed. I was at the Newport Folk Festival the year Bob Dylan went electric and half the audience went berserk with rage: you would have thought Moses had come down off the mountain with a Chinese restaurant menu.

In 1964 I heard recordings of the tenor Jussi Björling in *Pagliacci* and Maria Callas as Lucia di Lammermoor and there was no turning back; his tone was so plaintive and beautiful that I actually felt for the character, while she sounded like nobody I'd ever heard in my life and her emotions seemed primal. They made my body shake. A complete recording of Richard Wagner's *Die Walküre* followed—it was a very brave move—and I got caught up in the almost violent orchestra and the unbelievably huge, powerful voices that cut right through it. Could singing shock, bring sadness, amusement, and amazement, make one, as the composer Vincenzo Bellini said, "weep, shudder, die" and at the same time entertain, warm, and fill with joy?

And then in 1965 I actually went to the opera: *Die Walküre* at the old Met. My seat was the worst imaginable—in the "family circle," at the very top and over on the side—where you literally had to hang over the edge to see the stage, and it was only the front of the stage at that. My seat cost less than five dollars; a movie cost one dollar. The cast almost duplicated the one on my recording, and I found out a couple of years later that it was the greatest cast of the 1960s: George London was Wotan, Jon Vickers was Siegmund, Leonie Rysanek was Sieglinde, and Birgit Nilsson sang Brünnhilde. The opera was very long, and there were patches that confused and bored me (there were no subtitles to help in those days, and I wasn't familiar enough with the libretto), but the sheer sound and spectacle shocked me and made me almost hysterical; during the very late 1960s and all of the 1970s, I went to the opera (the Met and City Opera) three times a week. Without giving up my love for the Beatles, the Stones, the Who, the Beach Boys, Stevie Winwood (talk about a voice!), and the first syllable of Sting's "Roxanne," I have, since then, been loyally obsessed with the operatic voice. There's something so freakishly glorious about it, from bass to high soprano, that it demands a visceral reaction—anger, sadness, empathy, elation—and instant metaphor: dark, light, velvety, silvery, bell-like, chocolate, warm, golden, icy, laserlike, smooth. It is more like gospel singing than anything else, with many types of fervor in place of religious fervor. After a while singing seems like a natural extension of speaking; it's just another step up a communicative ladder.

To this day, I cannot understand why people don't sing—opera and otherwise—all the time.

Robert Levine

Introduction

NO NEED TO WEAR YOUR JEWELRY

This book is for anyone who has ever been curious about opera for any reason: whether you've discovered a sudden fondness for an aria used in a movie or an advertisement or an appealing singer seen on a billboard or a TV show, whether you've found yourself wondering how opera has lasted for more than four hundred years and seems to have recently caught on with new fervor, whether you want to know how to get into opera without causing any physical or mental harm to yourself or are simply tired of the singing on *American Idol*. Is opera a lifetime commitment, like marriage used to be? Are opera lovers like geese, mating with opera for life? Or is it—and can it be—an on-again, off-again thing? Why is it both mocked and perennially adored? If tickets are so expensive, how come everyone who loves it can somehow afford it? Why are there forty recordings of *Madama Butterfly* or *Don Giovanni*? Why do operagoers see—or listen to—the same opera dozens of times?

This book is also for people who want smarter babies, the ability to earn big bucks in their spare time, to take advantage of foreclosed properties, and to learn a foreign language and have flatter abs without leaving the comfort of their homes.

Remember what John Lennon said to an audience that included Queen Elizabeth, the Queen Mother, and Princess Margaret in November 1963: "For our last number, I'd like to ask your help. The people in the cheaper seats clap your hands. And the rest of you, just rattle your jewelry."

First of All . . .

Opera, simply, is sung drama, with the story told through both voices and instruments and often involving costumes and sets. It is like theater, in other words, except that the characters sing rather than speak. A group of late-sixteenth- and early-seventeenth-century Italians with money, status, and ideas believed that the plays of Greek antiquity, to which they aspired (the good old days?), had been sung rather than spoken. In fact, this belief was incorrect, but by the time everyone found out, opera had already taken hold, and an entirely new art form—and form of entertainment—had been invented.

The earliest operas used mythology and folklore as their subject matter; the first, now lost, is believed to have been about Dafne, a dryad, or nymph, who was turned into a laurel tree to protect her from the god Apollo. The music was by Jacopo Peri, Giulio Caccini, and Jacopo Corsi, and the opera was presented in Florence in the late 1590s at the suggestion of the poet Ottavio

Rinuccini, who rearranged the text from Ovid's *Metamorphoses*. *Orfeo* (about the mythical musician who goes to hell and back to retrieve his beloved Eurydice), by Claudio Monteverdi, was shown at the court of Mantua in 1607, and that's when opera really got started; *Orfeo* is still performed today. By 1637 Venice had opened the first public opera house, and by the century's end, that small city, with a population of 125,000, had seen 350 different operas in seventeen theaters. A typical "season" ran for from twelve to thirty weeks; the wealthy bought a box for the season; regular people bought tickets for individual performances.

As formulated by Monteverdi and his fancy friends, opera was made up, essentially, of two types of singing, the first being recitatives (as in "recite"), in which the characters, rather than singing a "song" about something specific, move the plot forward by singing their sentences to a written-out (not arbitrary) procession of notes that do not necessarily resemble a tune. This is the part of opera that initially makes people uncomfortable; musically pitched speech is abnormal. (In Broadway musicals, characters speak most of the time and then suddenly break into song. Why that should be less weird is beyond me, but there you have it. If you're going to sing at all, why not do it all the time?) A bit of dialogue in recitative might read: "I'm Apollo and I have slain a serpent and now I want Daphne." "Well, I'm Cupid and I'll turn her into a tree before you get your hands on her." The other type of singing in opera is the aria. These have tunes you can recognize (after a listen or two, as with any music), are more structured, stop the action, and focus on a particular feeling, event, or situation. "My girlfriend got bitten by a snake, now she's dead and I'm miserable, so I'm going to beg the infernal spirits to send her back" is a suitable reason for a full-blown song. (In the case of Monteverdi's *Orfeo*, I'm making this up, but you get the idea.) It may be strophic, in two parts—one filled with grieving, the other a statement of purpose, with more energy—or not, or more. An aria has a formality about it and literally calls a halt to the plot; even the earliest composers realized that the music of an aria had better be spellbinding, illuminate the situation, and keep the listener fascinated, because of its beauty or drama or the capability on the part of the singer to create beauty and drama—preferably both. Choruses pop up now and then to comment on the action, to be friends or witches or soldiers or rabble.

These basic elements—experimental works aside—that make up an opera are pretty much the same after more than four hundred years.

Thousands of operas were composed and performed during the eighteenth and nineteenth centuries (and into the first quarter of the twentieth), mostly in Italy, France, and Germany, and less so in England. (Opera houses also flourished in the United States in the nineteenth century, performing European works, but that is a story for another time.) Most people have heard of the still-popular composers, but for every Monteverdi, there were a few Cavallis and Caccinis; for every Handel, Lully, and Rameau, there was a gaggle of Kaisers, Grauns, Leos, Hasses, Bononcinis, Sarros, and Mondonvilles; for each Mozart, you could find a dozen Salieris; for each Bellini, Rossini, and Donizetti (the last of whom, alone, wrote almost seventy operas), there were plenty of Pacinis, Mercadantes, Mayrs, Payrs, and Meyerbeers; for each Wagner and Verdi and Mussorgsky, there was a handful of Marschners and Boitos; and for each Puccini and Richard Strauss there was a bunch of Mascagnis, Leoncavallos, Zandonais, Schillers, and Schrekers. Each town of any size had an opera house; some had several. If a new work did not please, it was replaced a night or two later by either an older, popular one or something new. Opera was *the* form of popular entertainment; the public took the characters and the music equally seriously. At the premiere of Gaetano Donizetti's *Lucia di Lammermoor*, people in the audience cried openly when the heroine went mad. We like to weep at "art"; it's a good way to reach inside without feeling we're getting too personal. A shared catharsis is a good thing, and in the case of opera, it is both diverting and private.

To mention just one example of opera's all-consuming presence, Giuseppe Verdi refused to give the orchestra or tenor the music to "La donna è mobile" (in *Rigoletto*) until the last moment because he was afraid that the tune was so catchy that the gondoliers would be humming it before the opening and spoil the surprise. Indeed, the morning after the premiere, everyone in Venice was singing it. Those who did not attend operas still heard the music, and they would sometimes adapt the melodies for home entertainment. Opera was an unavoidable and welcome fact of life, and though it may have attracted the rich and fancy, many seats were offered for the equivalent of pocket change. And the hoi polloi remained interested.

The interior of Teatro alla Canobbiana in Milan: Just one of the opera houses in Milan in the eighteenth and nineteenth centuries. Unlike the still-famous Teatro alla Scala, it catered to a middle-class audience.

So When and Why Did Opera Lose Its Place?

Opera retained its popularity into and through the first forty years of the twentieth century; indeed, opera singers were the celebrities of their day. It was the Neapolitan tenor Enrico Caruso

(1873–1921) who popularized the phonograph (and vice versa, it was said), making more than 260 recordings between 1904 and 1920; his records sold millions of copies, even to people who had never been to the opera. He was singing in San Francisco when the great earthquake hit in 1906; there were numerous stories about how he carried an autographed photograph of President Theodore Roosevelt with him for good luck as he was attempting to escape the city, which he did successfully, vowing never to return. Later that year, the new season at the Metropolitan Opera in New York was almost canceled when he was accused of pinching "Mrs. Hannah Graham's buttocks" at the Central Park Zoo's Monkey House. No Hannah Graham was found to live where the lady claimed to live, and she never appeared in court—she may merely have been one of the park's local loonies or may have been invented entirely by cops who were attempting to shake Caruso down. (Italian mobsters in New York also attempted to extort money from him.) The Met management came to his defense—the house was always full when Caruso sang, and they could not afford to lose him. He was eventually found guilty and fined ten dollars. Every newspaper covered the scandal; it was front-page news. New York's upper crust was horrified, but not enough to refuse to go hear him sing. And it wasn't just the fancy folk who flocked to hear him and bought his records. New York was filled with Italian immigrants—a half million of them—and they adored him and followed his every move. Each day of the trial, hundreds of Italians and Italian Americans had gathered at the courthouse, shouting "Viva Caruso!" whenever

CARUSO AS VASCO DI GAMA

The great Neapolitan tenor Enrico Caruso, probably not dressed for a tour of the Central Park Monkey House, where he was arrested for pinching "Mrs. Hannah Graham's buttocks."

the tenor entered or exited. Throughout his career he appeared in newsreels and silent films, although the two "romantic" films he made (and was paid $100,000 for) were flops.

More about the movies:

The soprano Grace Moore (1898–1947), from Slabtown, Tennessee (I'm not making this up), and almost a generation younger than Caruso, sang on Broadway and the opera stage. She was gorgeous, and when talkies came in she was just the right age and became as great a star in films as she was in opera. In her film roles she invariably portrayed an opera singer. The implication is not merely that she was photogenic (which she indeed was) and a good actress but that opera still had popular appeal. The tenor Beniamino Gigli (1890–1957), whose career rose to great supremacy upon the early death of Caruso (in 1921), made eighteen movies (in Italian, English, and German)—the films helped to sell the records and vice versa—and he was, despite not being particularly handsome, something of a matinee idol. He had an everyman type of charm (a 1950 film called *Taxi di Notte* cast him as a cabdriver who sings arias for extra tips). I'm sure you see where I'm going with this—people loved either opera itself or the idea of the opera singer. This was made crystal clear in the late 1940s and early '50s when a tenor, a young Philadelphian named Mario Lanza, born in 1921 but already singing professionally in the mid–1940s (he studied briefly with Leonard Bernstein), was heard at the Hollywood Bowl by the movie mogul Louis B. Mayer of MGM. Mayer signed him to a seven-year movie contract, and Lanza, with his good looks and gorgeous voice, became the everyday-hero-as-opera-singer. He crossed over perfectly, and his records sold millions of copies. His film *The Great Caruso*, released thirty years after the great Neapolitan tenor's death, revived—indeed, validated—what had been somewhat subjugated: the fact that opera could still sell to millions of regular Joes if delivered properly. Lanza's binge drinking and obsessive eating undermined his health, and he died at thirty-eight, after one of those induced periods of "twilight sleep." But that's another story.

By 1997 almost two dozen movie versions of *Carmen* had appeared, eighteen of *La Traviata*, thirteen of *Il Barbiere di Siviglia*, seventeen of *Tosca*, sixteen each of *Don Giovanni* and *Pagliacci*, fourteen of *Aida* (including one starring Gina Lollobrigida, lip-syncing the title role to Renata Tebaldi's voice), and thirteen each of *The Magic Flute* and *La Bohème*.

But . . . but . . .

A few things happened in the last half of the nineteenth and first quarter of the twentieth centuries, particularly in the United States and more particularly in the melting pot that is New York City. The American elite, those who had made it in the United States starting in the late eighteenth century and early nineteenth century, had divorced themselves from their European roots but, with their new wealth, opted to hang on to the "best" of European culture. Going to the opera—indeed, dressing for the opera and turning it into a place to be seen—became paramount, leaving the huge influx of financially struggling foreigners in the cold or at best in the peanut gallery, way upstairs in the opera house. The Academy of Music was founded in New York in 1854, and the opera season became the ne plus ultra of social life for the city's wealthy. The "best" (i.e., oldest and richest) families owned the seats in the theater's boxes, and this symbol of importance was passed from generation to generation. The Astors, Vanderbilts, Roosevelts, and Morgans were considered nouveaux riches and were therefore shut out of "society" and not permitted membership in the Academy. And so began internecine snobbism: the Metropolitan Opera Association in New York was founded in 1880 by just those "nouveaux riches" to counter this injustice, and when the new house opened in 1883 it held three tiers of boxes for the prosperous. At twice the size of the Academy, there was room for both New York society and the new immigrants and poorer opera lovers. This was practically democratic, although it should be noted with horror that there was a separate entrance for the two upper, cheaper, boxless tiers, presumably so that the new wealthy did not have to mingle with, or look at, those less well off and less well dressed. (The Academy of Music's opera seasons halted in 1886, and thereafter vaudeville and stage plays were presented there.)

At the same time and on the other hand, the newer immigrants wished to assimilate, and they leaned toward entertainment in their new language (or that needed little or no English, such as the silent movies), entertainment that was cheaper, entertainment that was easier to find. They bought Caruso's (and others') operatic recordings, but they listened to the radio and, by 1930, went to the movies, which were abundant. We know that opera translated relatively well to the movies, but westerns were newer; dramas were newer; slapstick comedies were newer. One cannot overemphasize the effect of close-ups on a huge screen; it is still what makes moviegoing "better" than theatergoing. Stars on the big screen started to take their places in the public's consciousness, stars more charismatic and invariably more glamorous than opera singers. Who could resist Greta Garbo, Clark Gable, Humphrey Bogart, Joan Crawford, Bette Davis, or Jean Harlow? Especially for fifteen cents, around the corner from where they lived? The more successful movies became, the more Hollywood turned them out, and opera began to lose its important place as entertainment for the people. Eventually, it became too much work and priced itself out of the common man's pocket. This explanation may seem simplistic, but it's probably right—and if it doesn't tell the whole story, it does help to explain why opera is reemerging. More on that in the next section.

Films eventually became more operatic than opera; in fact, everything became more operatic than opera. The early acting in silent movies is remarkable for its operatic excesses. Everything we now mock in opera—the hand-to-heart, hand-to-forehead emotionalism—was somehow considered exquisite at the movies. If, as we are told endlessly, opera is larger than life, then cinema is surely larger. Now the words "opera" and "operatic" have taken on meanings outside of any musical context. Critics write that Al Pacino gives "operatic" performances in *The Devil's Advocate* and *Scarface*. Francis Ford Coppola's *Godfather* trilogy and *Deadwood* by David Milch, the HBO series that ran for three seasons and takes place in South Dakota in the 1870s, have both been called operatic. So have the directors Brian De Palma, Clint Eastwood, and Martin Scorsese. And can anyone deny that Richard Pryor, every time he did stand-up comedy, was anything less than opera? It's not frequently referred to as "grand opera" for nothing; the "grand" refers to its emotional and presentational scope.

Opera became less of a necessity in everyday lives because everyday lives became more operatic. Joke about productions of *Aida* with elephants onstage if you'd like, but then take a look at the Grammys or go to a Rolling Stones, Elton John, or U2 concert. Where do you think such spectacle came from? It's the technology that has changed, not people's desire for glitz—which, incidentally, is now being seen in more and more opera houses.

So the Strange Thing Is . . .

The whole opera thing is coming full circle.

For most of our lives, opera has been gloriously easy to ignore. If you didn't want it or like it, you would almost never bump into it. A singer—usually Marilyn Horne or Beverly Sills—would occasionally show up on a late-night talk show or comedy series (*The Tonight Show, The Carol Burnett Show, The Odd Couple*) not only to dazzle with their voices but to demonstrate how down to earth they were. The Metropolitan Opera would broadcast operas on the radio on Saturdays during the winter and spring, but, for the most part, we were safe from exposure. Relatively frequent opera telecasts on PBS from the Met took hold in the 1980s and raised people's operatic consciousness, but let's face it, opera is grand and needs a stage—or screen—that is very big. (Between 1982 and 2002 the National Endowment for the Arts found that total attendance at live opera performances grew by 46 percent; one cannot rule out the power of television.)

By 1991, the phenomenon that was the Three Tenors made it clear that opera was for the masses and could be a hoot and, with their "friendly competition," a type of athletic event in itself (opera lovers have always seen opera as a sport, by the way—it ain't easy). Then the opera-wannabe-with-the-beautiful-voice, Andrea Bocelli, along with Pavarotti, Domingo, and Carreras, actually made millions of people enjoy opera, albeit in small doses. Just as the "chant" craze somehow appealed to the new age, rather than the religious, market, the Three Tenors suddenly became attractive to those who enjoyed stadium concerts. They were, after all, associating themselves with the World Cup, and it got blurred. Football, Pavarotti, Bruce Springsteen, Kiss— what's the difference? They're all over the top, they sing "hits" we recognize, and the crowd goes wild. The cult of the personality never hurts either—Pav's hugeness (in every way) made news, and there hadn't been a figure in opera so grand, so present, so "sensational" since Maria Callas, who had been in the headlines as much for her offstage exploits as for those onstage (*le jet set*; Aristotle Onassis; throwing tantrums; singing like an angel or a devil; canceling performances; and so on).

Then in 2006, in New York, came the Met's decision to telecast live opera in Times Square and in the Plaza at Lincoln Center, for free, on huge screens. Thousands upon thousands of people attended and sat rapt for three hours at a time, watching *Madama Butterfly* (with subtitles—now standard fare in opera houses as well) and liked it. Perhaps they came with memories of the Three Tenors ringing in their heads, but they now realized that opera was an "entire" thing and not just a series of well-known excerpts. Furthermore, they could follow it and enjoy it as if it were a movie or a TV show. Interviewed on the nightly news, dozens of people acknowledged that they had wept at *Madama Butterfly*. And remember—people love group crying, from *Lucia*

Mom Commits Suicide; Baby Waves Flag: The seduced and abandoned Madama Butterfly just postseppuku, with her half-American baby shielded from his mom's terrible fate.

di Lammermoor to the hysterical girls at early Beatles performances. Soon, not just the Met but La Scala in Milan, the Salzburg and Glyndebourne festivals, and other companies followed suit; in July 2009, ten thousand people gathered in London's Trafalgar Square to watch the Royal Opera's production of Verdi's *La Traviata*.

Finally, along came something crucial that proved that convenience plays a huge role in the way people of our century have learned to be entertained. Opera came to the proverbial "movie theater near you." With advances in digital technology, the quality of the projected films was vastly improved; something having to do with the number of pixels (please ask your local IT person or geek) makes the resolution of the picture sharper, realer, better. For about twenty-five dollars you get the entire experience, including, in some cases, intermission features (and you can get up and go to the bathroom when and if you need to). If people weren't going to the opera for one reason or another—too expensive, too dressy and glitzy (not necessarily anymore except in Germany, by the way), no wiggle room—opera would come to them. Going to the movies is a natural thing to do; going to the opera house had stopped being so. And in the United States alone, in 2009, more than a million tickets were sold for Met performances and people loved them. Neophytes, dazzled and comfy at once, went back for more, and fans found a new, cheaper, more convenient way for the music and theater to get to them and vice versa. And once you're hooked, you're hooked—opera becomes a sport of comparisons, heights, depths, and catastrophes; the movie-opera people are crossing over to the opera house and vice versa. Those who tell us that opera is a dying art form are simply off base—if it is dying, then it's been dying for four hundred years. Now we know that if it's easy to reach, people are interested; as Ray in the film *Field of Dreams* put it, "If you build it, [they] will come." There are now several distribution companies, all over the world, devoted to getting opera into movie houses. Opera is all around us—hundreds of hours' worth on YouTube alone—and there is no excuse not to take part in it. Much like the dozen or so theaters in eighteenth-century Venice (and then all over Europe), opera has again become familiar, popular entertainment, and it has unleashed its weird power. It still requires some commitment and knowledge and it rarely has a beat, but there's just so much of Lady Gaga a human being can enjoy/tolerate without needing to be touched in a slightly deeper place.

Yet There Are Still Some Philistines. Why?

Because opera is odd. Let me count the ways.

Everybody sings all the time, and that's not the way life is. I touched on this before, but it requires more discussion. We do raise and inflect our voices (except if we are from California or Oregon and especially if we are Italian, Jewish, or from the Deep South), but we stop short at singing. And it's too bad: raising one's voice is very effective. If instead of yelling when angry, we could sing at a good volume and at either a higher or lower pitch, and hold notes and words for a different period of time than normal, our points would come across more vividly. Yelling is just yelling; singing high is different from using a growling, lower sound. But I doubt that will happen, so let's get back to opera. My only advice for this issue is to get over it; if you love the human voice in any of its singing manifestations—Frank Sinatra, Sinéad O'Connor, Sting, Whitney Houston, Lady Gaga— you'll be turned on enough by opera singers to actually be glad that they sing all the time.

Opera does too many things at once. Going to the opera, or just listening to it, is multitasking: Should one detach the music from the drama? Is the voice preeminent? What if you don't like a particular voice—will that negate the experience? The answer is that it is a package. All of it is thrown at you at the same time (unless you are listening to recorded opera, which will be covered on page 27). If you don't like the sets, listen to the voices; if a particular voice grates, focus on the instrumentation, the action, or another singer. Keep your critical faculties sharp. In some ways it's no different from any theatrical experience: you may like one actor and not another; a director's approach may seem arbitrary or wrong or stupid or brilliant; the sets (or cinematography) may offend or please. But if you love John Travolta, you'll be predisposed to like any film he's in (except for that terrible piece of Scientology propaganda, *Battlefield Earth*; if you like that, please stop reading this book); if Quentin Tarantino is your cup of directors but you do not care for Travolta, you will probably still like *Pulp Fiction*. And if you love Giacomo Puccini's *La Bohème*, no production or singer can make you stop loving it. You'll just wish it had been better presented or sung. You can become a fan of a singer and not particularly like an opera he or she appears in at any one time.

Opera simultaneously envelops you and keeps you at a distance. In addition to being an aural and visual experience, it is emotional and cerebral, but it is *not* based in real behavior. Of course, neither is stand-up comedy—what is more fake than a man standing on a stage for the sole purpose of making you laugh while you drink? Who are you? Louis XIV? On some level it should have the opposite effect—"Just try to make me laugh, I dare you." But the audience is willing, and so it works; we meet the comic halfway, accepting the artificiality of the situation. Obviously, this is easy to get over, as the real tears that pour forth from many opera-goers will attest to. Trust me, if you let down your guard and give it an inch, it will take a foot. Consider opera entirely as metaphor, and its very artificiality will become one of its shining virtues.

Opera singers do not look like they sound. I'm not referring to the ever popular, ever tedious discussion of fat sopranos; many of them are extinct, and if you love and are moved by a particular voice, you can either get over the physique or joke about it, but the voice is what draws you in. What I'm referring to here is that if, say, Luciano Pavarotti's speaking voice had been as high as his singing voice, people would have begun to laugh every time he spoke. What comes out of most opera singers' heads is not a natural sound—it is one that is cultivated. Opera singers, except for basses and many baritones, sing in a range so much higher than anyone's natural speaking voice that making the connection between what you see and what you hear can be odd and difficult. This is certainly true of gospel singers as well, but for some reason, religious ecstasy is an acceptable reason for a high voice—period. Same with Whitney Houston (pre–Bobby

Brown). At this point, it is only rappers who sound "normal," but what they are doing is speaking in rhythm and rhyme, not singing. No offense—I speak the truth.

The plot does not really matter, Part I. A few years ago, as I was on my way to a performance of *La Traviata*, a non-opera-loving friend asked, "But haven't you seen it already?" In fact, I'd seen it a number of times, and yes, I knew what happened at the end. That isn't the point. If you recall that opera began with retellings of classical myths and stories, such as with Monteverdi's *Orfeo*, you'll realize that audiences were not attending to discover plot surprises. In the seventeenth century alone, there were composers, mostly forgotten today, such as Francesco Rasi, Antonio Brunelli, Stefano Landi, Luigi Rossi, Benedetto Ferrari, Giovanni Francesco Capello, and a dozen others, who set the Orpheus story to music; in total there are about sixty-five known operas on the subject. Clearly, the public wanted to hear how a particular composer treated the story, how effective the setting and music were, how moving the portrayal was. Add to that the infinite variety of singers who can sing the various composers' music with different sounds—no two voices are identical. The same is true in pop music as well, although we normally like the first version we hear best: it's considered "definitive." (Leonard Cohen's "Hallelujah," however, bears repeated listenings from many people.) In opera, unless it's a new work and we are at the premiere, it's hard to claim any definitiveness, but as your listening obsession becomes more sophisticated, you will have favorites as well. Still, a new production, a different Tosca, a different conductor, will whet your appetite and you won't be bothered by the fact that you know what's about to happen. It ain't what it does, it's what it sounds like.

The plot does not really matter, Part II. While some plots in opera fascinate and are utterly valid as theater (*Rigoletto, Pelléas et Mélisande, Der Rosenkavalier, La Traviata*), many are senseless or far too confusing, or have gaping holes in them (*La Forza del Destino, La Gioconda, Simon Boccanegra*). But that brings us to a crucial point about opera: although the overall scenario may be either trite or hard to believe, every opera worth its salt (hundreds of them in the standard repertoire) has many moments that rivet the listener as the simple spoken word simply cannot. So even though taken as a whole a plot can strain credulity, emotions are capable of being pinpointed in an aria or duet, say, not only by word but by sound of voice, range and reach of voice, and orchestral commentary/accompaniment. It is here that opera is actually hyperreal and larger than life. More about this later.

The plot does not really matter, Part III. "When someone gets stabbed in an opera, instead of bleeding, he sings." I'm not sure who said it first, but that says it all. And people have an issue with this—lengthy death scenes, tuberculosis victims with the lung power of longshoremen, slow-acting poison (and gunshots), the ability to sing beautifully and with great virtuosity for twenty minutes while insane, and so on. (I've just recently rewatched Quentin Tarantino's *Reservoir Dogs*, in which the actor Tim Roth screams, bleeds profusely, and dies for well over an hour; talk about operatic!) But again, please remember that opera is not supposed to mirror reality; it is supposed to depict emotional situations at their most heightened. Properly performed, and properly listened to, these finely tuned if unlikely—indeed, improbable—moments should and will transport us to a sphere way above our quotidian lives, to a place where we cry and/or shudder. If we can't get an emotion that strong out of any music we love, why listen to it? We get it from Jimi Hendrix, Sviatoslav Richter, a small group of pop or rock balladeers, and invariably from opera. Even Celine Dion has a voice that can send chills down the spine, and she's a Canadian robot.

Opera singers are overly temperamental. Sorry, but it is pop stars who demand bathtubs of Evian and crunchy chocolate health bars. Second of all, who cares if they are bratty—they're not your siblings, they're entertainers—but, more important, it is no longer true. The last twenty-five years have turned out not only fine singing actors but what used to be called troupers. The soprano Ana María Martínez, required to sing suspended from a wire in Antonín Dvořák's opera *Rusalka*, found that the least of her problems late in 2009 when she accidentally tripped onstage and fell into the orchestra pit, landing on a cellist. She got up and resumed singing. The American mezzo-soprano Joyce DiDonato slipped and broke her leg at London's Covent Garden in the midst of a performance of Gioacchino Rossini's *Il Barbiere di Siviglia*. She continued, and at the next few performances she sang from a wheelchair, occasionally shambling around in her cast. The baritone Simon Keenlyside accidentally fell through a trapdoor onstage, had surgery on his arm, and performed with a sling for a week or two. The soprano Danielle de Niese, in a production of Handel's *Giulio Cesare*, performed a knockout belly dance while singing a knockout aria at Glyndebourne. The words "diva" and "divo" (from the Latin for "goddess" and "god") are now kicked around to refer to any performer who is both wildly famous and demands a lot, but in any field of entertainment nowadays, if temperament outweighs talent, they're no longer tolerated. Two examples? Whitney Houston in pop and the unhinged Kathleen Battle in opera.

It's in a foreign language. Yes, it is. So is most of the world. Get over it. This is true of people from other countries, who are incomprehensible to us if they don't speak English. At least opera has subtitles in the opera house and on screens and you can buy a printed libretto to follow at home (most recordings include them anyway). Besides that, would it kill you to learn a phrase here and there in Italian, French, or German? But mostly: get over it.

Other Things You Should Know

Before we get to the operas proper—the plots, the history, the special "to die for" moments—we have a few more things to cover.

The first is the matter of relevance. There are whole groups of people who object to opera because they feel it should be relevant. To them, I say, Oh, please! What is "relevant"? Relevant to what? Today's news? People's habits? Even putting aside "gimmick" pieces for the moment (like the opera based on a Jerry Springer TV show), there have been plenty of so-called CNN operas— John Adams's *Nixon in China*, *The Death of Klinghoffer*, and *Doctor Atomic*; Michael Daugherty's *Jackie O*; Stewart Wallace's *Harvey Milk*; Anthony Davis's *X: The Life and Times of Malcolm X*; Ezra Laderman's *Marilyn* (that is, Monroe)—but the ones that have mattered to fans and press and have lasted through their first runs have been those in which the music illuminated the life or situation being treated. The *New York Times* wrote about *Marilyn*, "Musically, the opera's effect was often of an amiable lugubriousness." Monroe may be an obsession of yours, i.e., relevant to you, but does the *Times*' comment whet your appetite? Wagner's fifteen-hour Ring Cycle is considered a chore by those who do not love it, but it is musically and textually so rich that directors have rightly mined from it stories of power, lust, greed, psychological warfare, and familial dysfunction, sometimes by setting it in the future or present or at the time of the Industrial Revolution. Those things are relevant to us all, but they still should not be the reason we sit through and love the works. Do they speak to us in any deep-seated way, entertain us, and, perhaps, create that chill or make us tremble? If the answer is "yes," then they have relevance.

In addition, attempts to make standard operas relevant—or at least "modern"—tend to be embarrassing. German opera directors in particular have been at the forefront of what is called *Regietheater*, which translates as "director's theater" but is also often accused of being a type of intellectual Eurotrash. It implies a freedom in concocting the manner in which the opera is staged so that the composer's settings and dramatic intentions are often disregarded and often contradicted. At its best, say, in the director Patrice Chéreau's centennial production of the Ring Cycle at Bayreuth (Wagner's shrine, that is, the opera house he built for the sole purpose of presenting his operas), he underscored the Marxian, anticapitalist implications in the text at the time it was composed (the Industrial Revolution, as mentioned earlier). And Jonathan Miller's English National Opera production of *Rigoletto* was updated to New York's Little Italy in the 1950s, keeping the characters and their situations intact. But I have seen Puccini's *Madama Butterfly* removed from Japan and placed in a dirt garden, so that all of the characters are insects (Butterfly—get it?). In Munich, in 2005, *Rigoletto* was staged like *The Planet of the Apes*. In Berlin recently, a production of Christoph Willibald von Gluck's staid *Armide* included scenes of rape and bondage, not to mention a live python. In Cologne, Germany, half the cast left a production of Camille Saint-Saëns's *Samson et Dalila* because the violence made them sick, and when the curtain rose on Verdi's *Un Ballo in Maschera* in Barcelona a few years ago, the audience was treated to a row of men sitting on toilets, pants down, reading newspapers.

And one shudders at the following hideous examples: In September 2009 London's Royal Opera House presented "the world's first Twitter opera," based on almost one thousand tweets. It was called *Twitterdammerung*. The composer Curtis K. Hughes has written a work about Sarah Palin called *Say It Ain't So, Joe*, which features not only the fine lady but Vice President Joseph Biden and Joe the Plumber. Karl Marx's *Das Kapital* is being made into an opera in China, and London has already seen an opera based on the life of the *Playboy* model and celebrity Anna Nicole Smith. If the music of any of these works is good, I'll go, but what is your guess about the general quality of the ideas?

The second thing that comes to mind, and that you should pay attention to, is that opera is not for children, despite a recent

Sunday Times article, "Scottish Opera Stars to Perform Baby O for Infants":

> Scottish Opera is attempting to reach beyond its normal audiences of middle-aged music buffs by launching a series of concerts aimed at infants, aged between six and 18 months.
>
> The experimental performances, to be staged at venues across the country, will feature no lyrics, narrative or plot. Instead, classically trained singers will create baby-friendly noises, such as Wellington boots splashing in puddles, buzzing bees, quacking ducks and the fluttering of feathers.
>
> The audience will also be encouraged to gurgle along to the score and to crawl over a furry garden set, featuring hand puppets and a range of themed props.

I realize that this will upset the upwardly mobile parents who feel that if they introduce their toddlers to the finer things—Pablo Picasso's Blue Period, John Coltrane, *Nova*, the films of François Truffaut, artichokes, aged cheese, all thirty-three extant Vermeers, Mozart, and opera—then they will be giving them a leg up in a competitive world. The truth is that opera is surreal and artificial and in order to appreciate either surreality or artifice you normally have to know what art and reality are. Kids will sense that something is amiss, but they won't know what. They might tolerate *The Magic Flute* or *Hänsel und Gretel*, but only if the productions are colorful and zippy (and at least an hour of *The Magic Flute* is excised). Children like overkill, but not the type that opera normally offers. If you must, take girls to something sad (*La Traviata, Madama Butterfly*) and boys to an opera in which guys have fun and someone dies (*La Bohème*) or in which there are lust and death (*Carmen*). Warn them that opera is long, and make sure they can read (if they are below reading age and can't handle subtitles, have them watch it on TV if at all).

A Word or Two About Listening at Home

If you buy a CD or download an MP3 (or whatever), make sure you have a libretto. Read it first, previous to listening. Even before you actively listen (in a transitive way), put the recording on in the background; the music will seep in somehow. It will become familiar. Play it in the next room or while you shower—the big moments will come through. When you do actually listen, remember that it is not necessary to sit through a whole opera: listen in slices, and if you get bored, stop. Return later. Opera becomes urgent only once you love it; like anything you're learning—or that is worth exploring—it doesn't open itself completely the first time. Try to listen to an entire scene or act; if something catches your ear while it is in the background, stop and listen carefully to that few minutes. If you recognize an aria (from the Three Tenors or elsewhere), play it again, read along, and put it into context. Perish the thought, but if you find nothing you can latch onto in a specific work, try another, from fifty years earlier or later or from another country. You're developing your own tastes, and nothing you like will be wrong.

In this book, in a collection of the most renowned and memorable operas from different periods and countries, you will find interesting facts—some crucial, some silly, some gossip, all good for chatter during intermission—that fill out the general picture; plot summaries (just the basics); and a list of and brief dissertation on each opera's particularly spectacular moments. As we've seen, over the years opera has been taken away from "people" and mystified into something only the cleverest and richest can supposedly comprehend. The entire purpose of this book is to make listening and understanding opera an easier and less Byzantine experience: Of course, everything is better if you're rich and clever, but let's presume you're merely "comfortable" and somewhat on the ball and really like music and singing.

Now have a good time. Like chicken soup, opera is good for you.

German Opera

WHO'S AFRAID OF WAGNER
(AND HIS FRIENDS)?

German opera imitated Italian opera but also gave birth to the *singspiel*, a form that mixes spoken dialogue and sung arias, duets, and so on. Hamburg was an operatic hotspot in the late seventeenth and eighteenth centuries. Wolfgang Amadeus Mozart's operas *Die Entführung aus dem Serail* (1782) and *Die Zauberflöte* (1791) helped put German-language operas on the map, but there was nothing particularly German about them other than the fact that they were singspiels and in German. (Mozart, as you will see below, gets his own category/nationality, since he did not compose in any particular style other than Mozart style.) It was Carl Maria von Weber who introduced the supernatural and folk tunes and dances that put a true stamp on it. Then came Richard Wagner, and since then German opera is known to be long and heavily orchestrated.

Christoph Willibald von Gluck

Christoph Willibald von Gluck (1714–1787) was born in the Bavarian forest to a woodsman father—a setting more suited to a Grimm's fairy tale than to the future revolutionizer of operatic form. Of course, Gluck made it out of the woods (to hear him tell it, he sang for his supper along the road to Vienna) to Prague for university, and then on to Italy as his musical ambitions clarified. Those ambitions were lofty, to say the least. He aimed to do no less than transform opera. Breaking with the traditional and predictable series of recitatives and star-turn solo arias, Gluck felt that drama and story needed to come first. Singers should serve each piece's needs, rather than those of their fanatical fans. *Orfeo ed Euridice* premiered in 1762, and Gluck's "new style" rapidly became the style for contemporary opera. Over his career, Gluck was extremely prolific, composing more than thirty operas, as well as countless other works. Ironically (at least for those opera fans whose musical knowledge comes from fictionalized sources), Gluck was an important mentor to Antonio Salieri and was also influential on the young Mozart. Hector Berlioz deeply admired Gluck, who is also considered a precursor of that ultimate German opera man, Richard Wagner.

Orfeo ed Euridice (Orpheus and Eurydice)

Three acts
First performance: Burgtheater, Vienna, 1762
Libretto: Raniero de' Calzabigi

When Gluck set out to "reform" opera in the mid–eighteenth century, he did so with a vengeance. The traditions of *opera seria*, filled with subplots, disguises, and confused machinations, went against "good sense and reason," he claimed with some justification. With *Orfeo ed Euridice*, he altered those conventions. Gone were the singers' meaningless showpieces, the arias filled with brain-twisting metaphors, the endless volley of melodies having little to do with the text.

Orfeo's plot is both familiar and simple: as in the classical myth of Orpheus and Eurydice, Orfeo gets his chance to rescue his wife from the Underworld. Also as in the myth, there is a difficult requirement: Orfeo must not look back at his revived beloved—an impossible feat. However, the power of music is great and operates here as the spark that fires the culminating deus ex machina.

The opera's melodies are as direct as the story, and Gluck's emotional palette is equally straightforward. Dance and choral movements are fully integrated, not meaningless diversions. Of course, not all was exactly what modern-day listeners would think of as "natural": the role of Orfeo was composed for a castrato. When Gluck reworked the opera for Paris in 1774, he rewrote the lead part for tenor; nowadays the original version is the more frequently performed, with the role of Orfeo taken by either a mezzo-soprano or a countertenor. Whatever the voice range, the opera rises and falls on the singer in the role of Orfeo; it calls for a true singing actor. (The first Orfeo, Gaetano Guadagni, had taken lessons from the renowned Shakespearian actor David Garrick.)

Incidentally, I don't really consider this a German opera: it was set to an Italian text and first performed in Vienna. But since Gluck was German, here it is.

WHO'S WHO

Orfeo, a musician (contralto, countertenor or tenor)
Euridice, his dead wife (soprano)
Amor, God of Love (soprano)

WHAT'S HAPPENING

Greece, mythological time

Act I reveals Orfeo grieving by Euridice's tomb. Just as he makes up his mind to follow her fate, Amor, the God of Love, brings good news from Jupiter. Orfeo may descend in search of his wife, and if he plays his lyre pleasingly enough, he may bring her back with him. However: he must not gaze upon her until they return to the living world.

In Act II, Orfeo runs the gauntlet of the Furies, placating them with song. He sings again as the Happy Shades approach, and they present him with Euridice. Overjoyed, he takes her hand, careful not to look at her face.

Act III opens as Orfeo and Euridice commence their journey back into the world. However, she can't understand what seems to be his coldness and threatens to return to Hades if he does not look upon her. Distraught, he complies, and when he does so, she dies. Preparing to kill himself, Orfeo sings a lament so moving that Amor intervenes, bringing Euridice back to life and her long-suffering husband.

ACHTUNG! MOMENTS

This opera is very much a one-man (or -woman) show; the solo roles of both Euridice and Amor are brief, and Orfeo carries the opera. Each act contains superb—and very popular—orchestral moments such as the Dance of the Furies and the Dance of the Blessed Spirits (composed for Paris but frequently interpolated into any performing version), and the choruses, too, are of great interest. But the special moments noted below are those sung by Orfeo himself.

Act I: Orfeo's aria "Chiamo il mio ben così." Left alone, Orfeo, prepared to accept Euridice's death, expresses his grief. The aria is in three verses with dramatic recitative in between—a very odd, interesting touch.

Act II: Orfeo's aria "Che puro ciel." In Elysium, Orfeo sings of the purity of the air but finds no happiness in it; Euridice is still gone. Listen to the accompaniment in the orchestra—the delicacy and, yes, purity of the sound—particularly the oboe obbligato.

Act III: Orfeo's aria "Che farò senza Euridice?" This is the opera's most famous aria, sung after Euridice has died for the second time. It is a torrent of sadness in rondo form. Remarkable for its lack of decoration, it is in a major, rather than minor, or sad-sounding, key, but its very understatement makes it all the more poignant.

Ludwig van Beethoven

What is left to say about Beethoven? He was born in 1770 in Bonn, Germany, and his name practically means "greatness in classical music"; even people who have been living under a rock (and you know who you are) have heard of him and, moreover, heard some of his music, whether they know it or not. The finale of his Ninth Symphony has been used in hundreds of movies, TV shows, and advertisements; there are more than 250 available recordings of the work. In addition, he defines the moment when Classicism became Romanticism, when strict form could be bent somewhat to the benefit of self-expression. His music meant something: it could cry out for freedom, it could express joy or grief, it could explode aggressively, it could soothe.

We know that Beethoven moved from Germany to Vienna, where he studied with Joseph Haydn; we know that he was a piano virtuoso; we know he was unlucky in love; we know he began to go deaf in the 1790s (which might have been caused by a habit he had of submerging his head in ice-cold water in order to stay awake) and continued to compose until and after his hearing was entirely gone. By 1800 he was a great success, but eventually he had to stop concertizing because of the deafness; when he led the premiere of his Ninth Symphony, he had to be turned toward the audience at the end to appreciate the thunderous applause: he could hear none of it. And we know his hair always looked messy, that he was, in general, unkempt, and that he disliked and fought authority enough for Archduke Rudolf to state that the usual standards of court etiquette simply did not apply to him. He dedicated his Third Symphony to Napoleon Bonaparte, but when the little Corsican declared himself emperor, Beethoven scratched out the dedication with such vehemence that he tore the paper. To this day, Beethoven stands for freedom of the intellectual and creative spirit; when you listen to his music, you know the man behind its conception.

Fidelio

First performance of the original two-act version: Theater an der Wien, Vienna, 1805
First performance of the version we know today: Kärntnertortheater, Vienna, 1814
Libretto: Joseph von Sonnleithner

Fidelio, Beethoven's only opera, had a very long, difficult birth. Or, rather, a series of births. Its first version premiered in 1805 but was unsatisfactory; Beethoven quickly withdrew it and revised the piece. In 1806 he put forth a second version, with two rather than three acts, and in 1814 the temperamental maestro finally presented the version we know today. *Fidelio* is the most famous of what became known as "rescue operas," so named for obvious reasons.

The first two versions, rarely performed, are customarily referred to by the title *Leonore*. To add to the confusion, there are four overtures: the first, *Leonore No. 2*, debuted at *Fidelio's* premiere; *Leonore No. 3* is occasionally inserted before the opera's final scene (and opened the opera at its 1806 revision). Beethoven composed the *Fidelio* overture for the 1814 version, and now it always begins the opera. Finally, he wrote *Leonore No. 1* for a planned Prague production but subsequently dropped it. Confused yet? Forget about it. Each version (except for the unperformed *Leonore No. 1*) bears the stamp of Beethoven's passionate devotion to the concept of freedom. Fidelio is an odd work—the first half of the first act has the easygoing charm of a German singspiel—a light opera with dialogue—but the work turns dark, heavily dramatic, and truly Beethovenian with the entrance of Pizarro, the piece's villain, and continues with amazing power to the end. The finale has much of the power of his Ninth Symphony; it invariably brings audiences to their feet. And Leonore is opera's first real feminist.

WHO'S WHO

Leonore, in disguise as Fidelio (soprano)
Florestan, her husband, a Spanish nobleman (tenor)
Don Pizarro, prison governor (baritone)
Rocco, jailer (bass)
Jaquino, Rocco's assistant (tenor)
Marzelline, Rocco's daughter (soprano)

WHAT'S HAPPENING

Seville, eighteenth century

Florestan is supposed to be dead, but he is actually a political prisoner, held secretly by Pizarro in his fortress-jail. In Act I, his devoted wife, Leonore, in disguise as a young man named Fidelio, has taken a job as helper to Rocco. She easily wins favor with him; unfortunately, his daughter, Marzelline, is very attracted to the young man, much to the chagrin of Jaquino. It's an awkward and unfortunate situation, but Leonore perseveres, having learned that Florestan is confined in the deepest dungeon cell. Her mission becomes even more urgent when Pizarro, nervous at the pending arrival of the minister of state, announces that he will kill Florestan and bury him to destroy the evidence.

Act II opens upon Florestan, chained in his cell. Nearby are Rocco and Fidelio, digging his grave. Pizarro enters and draws his dagger, but Fidelio/Leonore pulls out a stolen pistol and steps between the two men. Leonore knows the truth and, to everyone's surprise, sings out, pointing to herself, "First kill his wife!" The minister arrives on the scene, recognizes his old friend Florestan, and gives Fidelio/Leonore the honor of freeing her husband from his bonds. Her determination, faithfulness, and willingness to face any danger tell the story of married love triumphant over all.

ACHTUNG! MOMENTS

Act I: The overture, a thrilling seven minutes that makes you remember what is so great about Beethoven; the quartet "Mir ist so wunderbar," a canon (think: "Row, row, row your boat") with a beautiful melody in which the characters express their feelings—a frozen moment that, in four minutes of stillness, takes the opera to a deeper emotional level; Leonore's aria "Abscheulicher!": She is alone onstage in this scene for the first time, and she sings with her whole range; previously, she has been with the others, disguised. Low, stabbing strings introduce her hatred of the villain, Pizarro, later turning into a prayerlike expression (with French horn solo) and then a faster section that lets us know how ferociously strong this character's devotion is. The voice rises to a triumphant high B on the words "married love."

Act II: Florestan's aria "Gott! welch' Dunkel hier!," a ten-minute psychodrama going from hopelessness to delusional hope and quite a workout for a tenor who's up to the work—note the mania with which he sings the word "Freiheit" (freedom) before he collapses with exhaustion; the quartet "Er sterbe!," in which Pizarro demands Florestan's immediate death and Leonore finally lets the others know who she is as she points a gun and screams, "Töt erst sein Weib" (First kill his wife); the duet "O namenlose Freude!," a brief, ecstatic moment for hero and heroine, with overlapping euphoric vocals, sung with something close to religious fervor. And, of course, the finale, which is life-affirming in the extreme. Awesome, in fact, dude.

Johann Strauss

The Viennese composer Johann Strauss II (1825–1899) was known as "the Waltz King" during his lifetime, and we should not hold this against him. There's really nothing wrong with "light music"; it was all the rage in late-nineteenth-century Vienna. His father was a well-known composer, and he wanted Junior to be a banker; Johann II began taking violin lessons on the sly before he was a teenager. When his father found out, he was enraged and tried to "beat the music" out of his son. It was not until Senior left the family for a mistress that Junior could devote himself to the study of the subject he loved. He formed an orchestra and began performing publicly at a casino in 1844. His work was immediately popular; his knack for melody and the Viennese love of waltzes made him famous. A father-son rivalry existed, however, made worse by their taking opposite political sides in the revolution of 1848. Upon Senior's death in 1849, Junior toured the Austro-Hungarian Empire, working himself into a nervous breakdown in 1853. Later, he toured Russia and the United States, gaining acclaim everywhere. Wagner admired him; Richard Strauss called him "the laughing genius of Vienna." It is easy to look down one's nose at his work but it's impossible to really dislike it. Start humming "The Blue Danube Waltz." Now try to get it out of your head.

Die Fledermaus (The Bat)
Three acts
First performance: Theater an der Wien, Vienna, 1874
Libretto: Karl Haffner and Richard Genée

Henri Meilhac and Ludovic Halévy supplied Jacques Offenbach with some of his most memorable texts. So when Johann Strauss came upon what would turn into *Die Fledermaus* (a French play called *Le Réveillon*), Strauss knew he would score a success.

Die Fledermaus is a light opera that has always attracted the "heaviest" of singers and conductors. Unlike some other operettas, which can be thrown together (at least theoretically) by a sincere semiprofessional troupe, *Fledermaus*'s vocal lines and orchestrations are so sophisticated that real pros are needed to perform it effectively. It was a favorite of conductors from Gustav Mahler to Richard Strauss, Bruno Walter, and Herbert von Karajan. It's the epitome of witty, refined comedy, and the characters and their easy-sounding but actually challenging music are both wacky and likable.

WHO'S WHO

Rosalinde (soprano)
Adele, Rosalinde's maid (soprano)
Eisenstein, Rosalinde's husband (tenor)
Alfred, Rosalinde's lover (tenor)
Prince Orlofsky (mezzo-soprano)
Dr. Falke (baritone)

WHAT'S HAPPENING

Vienna, c. 1850

In Act I, Falke wants to get even for a humiliating joke played on him following a party, wherein he woke up in broad daylight dressed as a bat. He invites the perpetrator, Eisenstein, to another soiree, planning some humiliations of his own. Meanwhile, Eisenstein tells Rosalinde he's off to serve a pending jail sentence (for insulting a tax collector!), but he's really heading for Prince Orlofsky's get-together with Falke. That leaves Rosalinde home alone with Alfred, an opera singer who has been wooing her. When the prison governor arrives, he mistakes Alfred for her husband and takes him off to jail.

Act II opens at Orlofsky's party. Everyone is wearing masks and getting befuddled, including Rosalinde's maid, Adele—and, most of all, Eisenstein, who flirts wildly with a woman he doesn't recognize as his wife (she's dressed as a Hungarian countess).

Act III unfolds in and around the jail, where true identities come to light, indiscretions are forgiven, and everything can be conveniently blamed on the revenge of the Bat.

ACHTUNG! MOMENTS

Act I: The trio "So muss allein ich bleiben," a comedy of errors, which manages to be both cynical and enchanting at the same time.

Act II: Adele's aria "Mein Herr Marquis," also known as the "Laughing Song" for the high, coloratura laughter the soprano is called upon to produce; Rosalinde's czardas (a traditional Hungarian folk tune), "Klange der Heimat"; "Brüderlein und Schwesterlein," led by Falke, a veritable poem to love and loyalty.

Act III: There is actually more spoken dialogue than music in this act, but the trio "Ich stehe voll Zagen" is a pip.

Engelbert Humperdinck

Nowadays known only for *Hänsel und Gretel* (despite his 1897 *Die Königskinder* being a hit at the Met for a few seasons in the early part of the twentieth century), Engelbert Humperdinck (1854–1921) was somewhat of a child prodigy, composing little operas with dialogue (singspieles) when he was thirteen. He traveled widely, and in Naples he met Richard Wagner; the older composer invited him to Bayreuth to help with the production of *Parsifal* in 1880. At the same time, he tutored Wagner's son, Siegfried (who later composed many overblown operas), and actually composed a small bit of music for *Parsifal* that was needed when a scene change went on too long. Richard Strauss led the first performance of *Hänsel*, declaring it a masterpiece. He was right. And please do not confuse this fine composer with the inexplicably popular lounge singer of the 1960s and '70s of the same stage name, who was born Arnold Dorsey and was a poor man's Tom Jones.

Hänsel und Gretel
Three acts
First performance: Hoftheater, Weimar, Christmas 1893
Libretto: Adelheid Wette

Hänsel und Gretel's story is little changed from the well-known Grimm brothers tale, with clever children outwitting the cannibalistic witch and a house that's so delicious that it almost becomes a character in itself. Musically, however, Humperdinck blends an uncanny mixture of Wagnerian technique and orchestration with folksiness and naiveté.

The work's genesis might explain the contradictions. Adelheid Wette lived in Cologne with her husband and two daughters. Her younger brother, Max, built a puppet theater for the girls, and they put on plays, many based on the Grimms' fairy tales. Adelheid wrote the texts for these little theatricals, and, because the girls loved to sing, their mother asked her older brother to set her lines to music, which he did, occasionally using folk tunes. This brother, Engelbert, had worked as an assistant on the first performance of Wagner's *Parsifal*—as good training as can possibly be imagined for a career as an opera composer. The resulting piece, *Hänsel und Gretel*, was a post-Wagnerian composition with an innocent touch and a wildly popular opera for sophisticates and novices alike. Within a few years of its premiere, it had been translated into eleven languages.

WHO'S WHO

Hänsel (mezzo-soprano)
Gretel, his sister (soprano)
Peter, their father, a broom maker (baritone)
Gertrud, their mother (soprano)
Witch (mezzo-soprano)
Sandman (soprano)
Dew Fairy (soprano)

WHAT'S HAPPENING

German mountains, fairy-tale time

In Act I, Peter returns home to hear that Gertrud has unwittingly sent Hänsel and Gretel into the witch's woods. In Act II, the children realize they are lost, and they are frightened until the Sandman appears with his blessing of sleep. Act III brings the dawn and the Dew Fairy, but soon the children are on their own. Of course, they can't resist the gingerbread house that has appeared before their eyes. When they begin to nibble, the witch invites them in and casts her spell. Gretel breaks it by finding the witch's magic wand, and she and Hänsel push the witch into her own oven—just what she was planning to do to them! The oven explodes, the spokes of the gingerbread fence turn back into children, and the parents arrive in time to share a big witch cake.

ACHTUNG! MOMENTS

Act I: The duet "Brüderchen, komm, tanz mit mir," a rollicking dance duo for the kids.

Act II: The Sandman's song; Hänsel and Gretel's prayer "Abends will ich schlafen gehn"; the orchestra-only dream pantomime.

Act III: The Witch's spell "Hokus pokus, Hexenschuss!"

Richard Strauss

The Munich-born Richard Strauss (1864–1949) changed the operatic world with *Salome*. Considered by many critics to be the epochal first work of twentieth-century Modernism, the piece quite literally pits the past and the future of tonality against each other. Salome's music is strange and convoluted, while John the Baptist's is mainly in straight major keys. Though this may seem rather lofty for the average listener, consider it this way: Picasso never painted a picture in which one character was finely drawn, as in his Blue Period style, and the other a total Cubist distortion. Strauss does just that, only in music. Still more fascinating, Strauss was as capable as any composer before or since of writing a straight-ahead, fun-for-the-whole-family piece of operatic confection. His *Der Rosenkavalier* is as delightful, funny, and socially pointed a work as any since *The Marriage of Figaro*. But with *Salome* he was out to get people's attention, and he certainly did. Late in his life, a story goes, he got into a taxi in Salzburg and the driver, recognizing him, asked, "Where to, Herr Strauss?" "It doesn't matter," Strauss answered. "I'm in demand everywhere."

Salome

One act
First performance: Hofoper, Dresden, 1905
Libretto: Adapted by the composer

The New Testament story of Salome could well be subtitled "Hell hath no fury like a woman scorned." Infamously, of course, the scorner is Jochanaan, better known as John the Baptist, whose piety makes him morally immune to the beautiful sinner's charms.

After the public and critical disapproval of his previous operas *Guntram* and *Feuersnot*, Strauss began to be seen as a rebel. One of his journal entries reads, "It's unbelievable what enemies *Guntram* has made . . . I shall shortly be put on trial as a dangerous criminal." Of course, the composer was exaggerating at that time. However, with his next opera, *Salome*, based on a play by none other than Oscar Wilde, his reputation as a blaspheming scandal maker was assured.

When New York's Metropolitan Opera presented *Salome*, it had to be withdrawn after a single night. Apparently, that single performance was enough for one reviewer to write, "*Salome* is a detailed and explicit exposition of the most horrible, disgusting, revolting and unmentionable features of degeneracy that I have ever heard of, read of, or imagined. . . . Strauss's music is aesthetically criminal." The upshot of the controversy? There were productions of *Salome* in fifty different opera houses within the next two years. Frankly, its overt depiction of a deranged teenager's libido coupled with Strauss's raucous-but-ravishing orchestration still leaves audiences disturbed.

WHO'S WHO

Salome, Princess of Judea (soprano)
Jochanaan, or John the Baptist (bass-baritone)

Herod, King of Judea (tenor)
Herodias, Salome's mother (mezzo-soprano)
Narraboth, the captain of the guard (tenor)

WHAT'S HAPPENING

Galilee, c. A.D. 30

Salome, the stepdaughter of Herod, becomes entranced by the
voice of Jochanaan, prophesying from his dungeon. She seduces
his guard, convincing him to bring the prisoner up to her. Jochanaan denounces Salome's mother, the queen, for killing her
husband in order to marry Herod, and also he rejects Salome's
every advance. Even so, her lust for him grows, driving her nearly
insane. She pretends to accept the advances of her stepfather,
Herod, who, more and more lascivious, promises her anything
she wants in return for a dance. After performing the Dance of
the Seven Veils, she demands John the Baptist's head. Herod reluctantly complies, and she revels in her prize, kissing the severed
head as her mother laughs her approval. Herod, sickened by the
scene, orders Salome crushed to death by his soldiers.

ACHTUNG! MOMENTS

Salome is only 100 minutes long and very tightly constructed.
Like a Wagnerian opera, it is difficult to excerpt, difficult to pick
highlights from. But one of its more enthralling moments is Jochanaan and Salome's scene in which the more revolted he is by
her, the more she wants to touch his skin, hair, and lips, beginning with the words "Wo ist er."

Salome's Dance of the Seven Veils, a nine-minute sensual explosion for Strauss's exotic orchestra; the demented final scene, a Salome solo, in which she finally gets to kiss the severed head: "Ah! Du wolltest mich nicht deinen Mund küssen lassen."

Der Rosenkavalier (The Knight of the Rose)
Three acts
First performance: Königliches Opernhaus, Dresden, 1911
Libretto: Hugo von Hofmannsthal

In both *Salome* and *Elektra*, Strauss had examined perverse female obsessions, hysterical dancing, and hideous deaths. With his next opera, *Der Rosenkavalier*, he continued his fascination with women and the female voice—but did a 180-degree turn emotionally and psychologically. In this fun and funny opera, an older woman (about thirty-five, by the librettist's instructions) realizes that she must give up her young (i.e., teenage) lover for his own—and her own—good. As psychologically heavy as that may seem, it is treated with such grace, and such oddly slapstick humor, that it never adversely affects the delightful whole. Some people—and I count myself among them—find this opera bloated: the funny bits in the second and third acts go on for too long (each act is a bit over an hour long), but there is no denying how gorgeous the gorgeous bits are (see below).

Der Rosenkavalier features three star female voices (Octavian is a travesti, or "pants," role—Strauss's answer to Mozart's Cherubino, he claimed). *Der Rosenkavalier*'s vocal lines soar gracefully rather than violently, and in place of the anguish of the two earlier operas, we are given nostalgia, generosity, humor, and a smile toward the future. And what of the frenzied dancing? Richard Strauss has replaced it with waltzes worthy of that other Strauss, Johann.

WHO'S WHO

The Marschallin, Princess von Werdenberg (soprano)
Baron Ochs, the Marschallin's cousin (bass)
Octavian, the Marschallin's young lover (male role played by mezzo-soprano)
Herr von Faninal (baritone)
Sophie, his daughter (soprano)

WHAT'S HAPPENING

Vienna, mid-eighteenth century

In Act I, the loutish Baron Ochs barges in on the teenage Octavian and the married Marschallin moments after a night of hot lovemaking. Octavian disguises himself as a chambermaid, and Ochs himself is enticed. But Ochs is engaged to the young, lovely Sophie, and he has really come in search of a cavalier to present to her the traditional silver rose of engagement. The Marschallin offers Octavian's services, and in Act II, Sophie and Octavian meet and fall instantly in love. She is naturally now even more appalled to meet Ochs, her future groom. To save the young beauty, Octavian duels with Ochs, whose slight wounds are healed by the promise (through paid intermediaries) of a second meeting with the luscious "maid." As Act III unfolds, Octavian exposes Ochs's roguery to Sophie's father, who breaks the marriage contract. Now Octavian must face the Marschallin. She has known this would one day happen, so she sends her lover into the younger woman's arms.

ACHTUNG! MOMENTS

Act I: The Marschallin's monologue "Da geht er hin," which she sings after Octavian has exited. It is a few minutes of great introspection and honesty in which she faces her own aging: "Sometimes at night, I awaken and stop all the clocks."

Act II: Presentation of the silver rose, "Mir ist die Ehre widerfahren," in which the vocal lines for mezzo-soprano and high soprano intertwine with luscious, sensual harmonies; Ochs's "Ohne mich, ohne mich," a waltz song that both captivates and amuses, bringing the act to a very Viennese end.

Act III: The trio "Marie Thérèse," in which the lovers unite and the Marschallin comments from the sidelines—perhaps the most divine trio for women's voices ever written.

Alban Berg

It is hard to imagine a composer whose work so embodies the decadent, grotesque, and phenomenally creative Weimar era as Alban Berg (1885–1935). This is ironic, because Berg was actually Viennese through and through: he was a student and protégé of Arnold Schoenberg, a follower of that master's twelve-tone atonal composition technique, and a friend of Viennese artists including Gustav Klimt. Somewhat unfairly, Berg's music is often pegged as "hard" listening. *Wozzeck* can be a difficult proposition, at least for subscription audiences more attuned to *La Bohème* or *La Traviata*. This assessment leaves out the sheer dark thrill of hearing—and seeing—something so purely and entertainingly modern on the opera stage. Arguably, *The Three-penny Opera* would not exist without *Wozzeck*, nor might a host of other works both creepy and, well, atonal: Benjamin Britten's *The Turn of the Screw* and Dmitri Shostakovich's *Lady Macbeth of the Mtsensk District* come to mind. Berg died young of blood poisoning from an infected boil on his back. Not surprisingly, he was loathed by the Nazis, who considered all modern music to be the work of filthy undesirables. Maybe if he had survived, Berg would have followed Schoenberg and his other Mittel-European atonal friends to the postwar paradise of Hollywood. Alfred Hitchcock would have loved him.

Wozzeck

Three acts
First performance: Staatsoper, Berlin, 1925
Libretto: Adapted by the composer

Ten years elapsed between the time Berg saw the play *Woyzeck* by Georg Büchner and the premiere of his opera based on it. The story was a perfect foil for the composer's darkest instincts and the Weimar era in which it was composed: the not-too-bright soldier Wozzeck must endure lectures on immorality from his insane captain; worse, he must undergo experiments by the doctor for money to support his companion, Marie, and their illegitimate son. When he discovers that Marie has been unfaithful, his already tormented mind snaps, and everything ends in a wash of blood.

This is the peak of Expressionism in music. When *Wozzeck* finally premiered, it was like a thunderbolt across the operatic world. Despite the fact that the opera is very formally composed—there are a fugue, a symphony in five movements, a sonata, and a passacaglia—the atonality of the music and immorality of the libretto both shocked and horrified its audiences. One critic, referring to the piece's odd sounds, called Berg "a Chinaman from Vienna," adding that the opera was "a deliberate swindle . . . fragments, sobs, belches . . . an ugly-sounding cackle." The reviews continued to be so hysterical that Berg's publisher had them bound in a little volume and distributed! The next year, a production in Prague started a riot during which the mayor died of a heart attack. Although the last hundred years have heard music far more peculiar, aggressive, and difficult, to this day many people become excessive when they speak of Berg's music. Like it or not, sitting through an evening of *Wozzeck* packs a theatrical, musical, and emotional wallop you won't soon forget.

WHO'S WHO

Franz Wozzeck, a soldier (baritone)
Marie, his common-law wife (soprano)
Marie's son (treble)

Drum Major (tenor)
Captain (tenor)
Doctor (bass)

WHAT'S HAPPENING
Leipzig, 1824

In Act I, Wozzeck undergoes his daily trials with the captain and the doctor. Constantly distracted, he fails to give Marie the attention she craves, and she gives in to the advances of the drum major.

In Act II, Wozzeck discovers her infidelity. Suffering from the taunts of the captain, the doctor, and the drum major, Wozzeck hallucinates about a knife.

In Act III, Marie repents, but to no avail: Wozzeck takes her into the woods and cuts her throat. He later returns to the pond into which he threw the knife and walks into the water himself, going deeper and deeper until he drowns. Marie and Wozzeck's child, unable to comprehend the loss of his parents, plays on his hobbyhorse as the final curtain falls.

ACHTUNG! MOMENTS
Unexcerptable—just digest the ninety minutes in one sitting. By the time of the orchestral interlude near the opera's end, you will either have left your seat or be figuratively nailed to it.

Richard Wagner

More has been written about Richard Wagner (1813–1883) than anyone except Jesus Christ. (I realize this sounds like a joke, but it is not.) One of the most complicated, brilliant, and disagreeable men in the history of music, he caused, essentially, a one-person revolution in opera. He was the Platonic ideal of musical fascism, taking into account every aspect—the music, words, staging, settings, and lighting—of every work he created. Halfway through his career, King Ludwig II of Bavaria discovered him, and the monarch, half mad, obsessed with ancient Greece and the Italian Renaissance, a terrible poet, addicted to candy (his teeth were entirely rotted by the time he was in his forties), and most likely in love with Wagner—unrequitedly—funded Wagner's undertakings. The composer was ultimately able to found his own theater (with a covered orchestra pit), in which only his operas would be performed in the town of Bayreuth, Germany; to this day the "Wagner Shrine" is home to a festival of the composer's works, which is sold out at least seven years in advance. A supreme narcissist, he was endlessly borrowing money he had no intention of repaying, and he had no second thoughts about stealing another man's wife (his second wife, Cosima, was the wife of his friend the pianist, teacher, and conductor Hans von Bülow when Wagner and she began their affair; she was also the daughter of Franz Liszt); nor was he shy about his anti-Semitism. This last trait made him Adolf Hitler's favorite composer and the unofficial musical voice of the Third Reich. To this day many people have trouble separating the man Wagner from the composer Wagner. It's easy: forget about the former and listen to the music that has been transporting people to other realms for more than 150 years.

Maurice Renaud as the happy-go-lucky Dutchman, looking for a woman to save him. Good luck.

Der Fliegende Holländer (The Flying Dutchman)

One act, occasionally performed with two intermissions, one after each scene
First performance: Königliches Sächsisches Hoftheater, Dresden, 1843
Libretto: Written by the composer

The legend of the Flying Dutchman—a sailor doomed by Satan to sail the seas forever for making a foolish oath—was immensely popular in Europe in the first part of the nineteenth century. Wagner had read Heinrich Heine's *From the Memoirs of Herr von Schnabelewopski* (1834), in which the title character attends a play about the Dutchman. There is a good chance that Heine himself had seen an 1826 play of the same name by Edward Fitzball, who'd probably read an anonymous story on the subject in a magazine in 1821. Then there was *The Phantom Ship*, an 1839 novel by Captain Frederick Marryat about a Dutch sea captain . . . and so on. The curse allows him to go ashore once every seven years and search for a woman who will be true to him until death—this is his only hope of salvation. At any rate, Wagner's opera appeared in 1843, with Heine's setting changed from Scotland to Norway and the concept of a woman's sacrifice through death deepened. The piece put a fittingly Wagnerian finish on the spate of doomed-sea-captain tales. And ever since, when we think of such a character, it is invariably in Wagner's incarnation.

WHO'S WHO

The Dutchman (bass-baritone)
Daland, Norwegian sea captain (bass)
Senta, Daland's daughter (soprano)
Erik, Senta's suitor (tenor)

WHAT'S HAPPENING

The Norwegian coast, the nineteenth century

In the first scene, the Dutchman and Daland, both sea captains, make a deal when the Dutchman hears that Daland has a marriageable daughter and Daland sees the riches on the Dutchman's ship. Scene ii introduces Senta among her friends; she daydreams about the legendary Dutchman—whose picture hangs on her wall—and she longs to be the woman who sets him free. Erik warns her of the danger of her weird behavior, but when Daland returns with the Dutchman, Senta realizes he is the incarnation of her obsession and she and the Dutchman pledge love until death. In the final scene, as Erik is again attempting to woo and talk sense into Senta, the Dutchman sees them and thinks she has gone back on her word to him. He races off to set sail alone. She sees his ship depart and flings herself into the sea, thus proclaiming her faithfulness. The ship sinks and the spirits of the Dutchman and Senta rise from the waters, heaven-bound.

ACHTUNG! MOMENTS

The overture—one of the great depictions of the sea and a disturbed mind in all of music.

Scene i: The Dutchman's entrance scene, "Die Frist ist um," in which we learn everything about him in ten minutes: he is damned, depressed, and, except for a glimmer, hopeless. A staggering psychological profile. Part of the score is marked *agitato*: an undulating theme elsewhere mirrors his constant wandering.

Scene ii: Senta's ballad "Traft ihr das Schiff im Meere an." Also known as "Senta's Ballad," this aria, is, in some ways, a grand hallucination and, in addition to taxing the soprano, gives us quite a picture of this neurotic girl. Strings whistle like the wind at the start of each verse.

Scene iii: The chorus of Norwegian and Dutch sailors: a thrilling back-and-forth that starts out as fun and ends with the Norwegians' terrifying realization that the Dutch seamen are zombies. The finale, "Verloren! Ach, verloren!" (Lost! Lost! All hope of salvation lost!): with wild downward string figures and blasts from the brass, the Dutchman bursts onto the scene and denounces Senta; she attempts an explanation, and Erik expresses horror at Senta's behavior in this marvelous, very Italianate trio. Senta hurls herself into the sea. It may sound silly, but it is musically gripping.

Lohengrin
Three acts
First performance: Großherzogliche Hoftheater, Weimar, 1850
Libretto: Adapted by the composer

In 1845, Wagner had just completed his opera *Tannhäuser* and was overwrought—as usual. His physician prescribed the waters at Marienbad Spa, as well as absolute mental rest. Unfortunately for his emotional state, but to the benefit of opera lovers until the end of time, Wagner took with him on his rest cure an anonymous epic about Lohengrin, the son of the knight Parsifal. As the composer himself later reported, he took the book with him into the medicinal baths one day, and it was there, in complete relaxation, that he had a vision of how to treat the legendary story operatically. Leaving the bath immediately, Wagner returned to his rooms and wrote the synopsis of *Lohengrin*—in almost the exact form we know today.

Lohengrin is Wagner's most Italianate opera—there are set arias, duets, and ensembles. It also contains some of his most beautiful—and approachable—music and is the Wagner opera for people who normally don't like Wagner operas. The delicate character of Elsa and her dreamy, lovely music is matched by that of her hero, Lohengrin, who has the most sheerly beautiful music Wagner ever wrote for tenor. The dramatic mezzo-soprano (or soprano) role of Ortrud is unique in Wagner—a truly monstrous bitch, devoted to cruelty—with not one but two wild outbursts that are so aggressively voice-wrecking that they tend to stop the show—in a good way. The subject matter is, again, superficially outlandish and based on impossibilities (see below: knight on swan-drawn boat, swan = prince, etc.), but the basic issues—trust, malevolence, unconditional love—are nothing to sneeze at.

WHO'S WHO

Lohengrin, a knight of unknown origin (tenor)
Elsa, Princess of Brabant (soprano)
Friedrich von Telramund, Elsa's uncle and guardian (baritone)
Ortrud, Telramund's pagan wife (mezzo-soprano)
Heinrich, King of Germany (bass)

WHAT'S HAPPENING

Antwerp, tenth century

In Act I, Elsa is blamed unjustly for the mysterious disappearance of her brother. Her innocence or guilt will be decided by combat, but there is no one to champion her side. She recounts a dream she's had about a knight who rescues her. Suddenly, in a riverboat drawn by a swan, a knight in silver armor appears, offering to be both her protector and her future husband. Accepting, she promises to obey his one command: she must never ask his name or his history. A duel ensues, and the unknown knight beats Telramund, the accuser.

The start of Act II spotlights the evil Ortrud and her weak husband, Friedrich von Telramund. They have already stolen the dukedom belonging to Elsa's brother and must now rout the popular knight by spreading rumors about his past. Ortrud feeds Elsa's curiosity and innocence, but the wedding takes place anyway. At the start of Act III, after their wedding, the anxious Elsa puts the forbidden questions to her brand-new groom. When Friedrich breaks in, Lohengrin kills him and declares that he must go before the king to answer the questions asked by

GEGRÜSST DU GOTTGESANDTER HELD! SEI GEGRÜSST!

Lohengrin, sword at the ready, arriving by swan-drawn boat. A little showy, I'd say, but public transportation in tenth-century Antwerp wasn't what it should have been.

his bride. Revealing that he is Lohengrin, a knight of the Holy Grail, he then transforms his swan into the human form of Elsa's brother, a victim of Ortrud's spell. All rejoice, but too soon: Lohengrin, exposed, must now depart, and Elsa dies on the spot.

The moral of this story: don't ask your knight in shining armor too many questions.

ACHTUNG! MOMENTS

The Prelude to Act I: Simply heavenly music, with divided strings sounding like angels.

Act I: Elsa's hypnotic, hopeful dream, "Einsam in trüben Tagen"; Lohengrin's entrance, "Nun sei bedankt," a tender, loving ode.

Act II: The vicious opening duet between Ortrud and Telramund; the Elsa-Ortrud scene "Euch Lüften," during which Ortrud wheedles her way into Elsa's confidence; Ortrud's maniacal curse, "Entweihte Götter!"; the wedding procession.

Act III: The Prelude; the bridal chorus (the famous melody to "Here comes the bride / All dressed in white"); Lohengrin's narrative "In fernem Land," in which he describes his origins. This, and his farewell, are two of the finest moments in early Wagner and probably the most handsome music he ever wrote for tenor: a combination of the lyric and heroic, with long melodies. A brief, totally crazy outburst from Ortrud comes right near the opera's close, and it's an unforgettable eruption.

Die Meistersinger von Nürnberg
(The Mastersingers of Nuremberg)

Three acts
First performance: Hoftheater, Munich, 1868
Libretto: Written by the composer

Having finished *Tristan und Isolde*, Wagner decided to revisit a subject he had prepared in 1845, a comedy about a Guild of Mastersingers that actually existed in Germany from the fourteenth to sixteenth centuries, whose goal was maintaining the purity of the German song. His hero was to be a real sixteenth-century character, Hans Sachs, a wise, loving cobbler who had written some 6,000 poems and 4,000 songs. Wagner's music is vivid and shining, with none of the gloom that he was so good at laying on; the themes of young love and the elderly Sachs's generosity are what matters. Well, what also mattered to Wagner was made clear in his libretto: he wanted "holy German art" to be free of outside influences. More often than not, when Sachs sang those words in performances in Germany from 1938 to 1944, the audience rose and gave the Nazi salute; it spoke directly to their nationalism/racism. Moreover, the character of Sixtus Beckmesser, the fussy, traditionalist "marker" (the person who made a mark on a blackboard when an auditioner made an error—the Mastersingers had a list of thirty-two flaws in the art of singing that must be avoided), was modeled by the composer after the half-Jewish Eduard Hanslick, a leading critic of the time known for his conservative views—which included a dislike of Wagner's music. Though often narrow-minded ("For my heart, music really begins with Mozart and culminates in Beethoven, Schumann, and Brahms," he wrote), he was undeniably an excellent critic. However, his excellence didn't interest Wagner, who saw in Hanslick everything he pictured himself fighting against—both politically and socially. Nationalism in opera is not a rarity, but Wagner could be toxic, and, comedy or not, a four-and-a-half-hour show in which the point of view (or at least the subtext) is decidedly xenophobic is bothersome. But *Die Meistersinger*, for all its longueurs, is a wellspring of melodies, with rousing choruses, great pageantry, and truly touching moments.

WHO'S WHO

Hans Sachs, a cobbler and poet (baritone)
Eva (soprano)
Veit Pogner, Eva's father (bass)
Walther von Stolzing, Eva's suitor (tenor)
Sixtus Beckmesser, town clerk and marker and Walther's rival (baritone)
Magdalena, Eva's nurse (mezzo-soprano)
David, Sachs's apprentice and Magdalena's boyfriend (tenor)

WHAT'S HAPPENING

Nuremberg, sixteenth century

In Act I, Walther spots Eva at church, and when they meet, they fall in love. Because her father, Pogner, has promised her hand in marriage to the winner of the Mastersingers' song contest, Walther auditions for membership (the apprentice, David, tells him the rules)—to the jeers of all except Hans Sachs.

Act II begins with Walther and Eva trying to elope. Madgalena, disguised as Eva, is serenaded by Beckmesser, which enrages her boyfriend, David, and Sachs critiques the performance with mocking hammer blows to a shoe he is supposedly repairing: he plays the "marker." He also prevents the ill-conceived escape of the lovers (and manages to suppress his own love for Eva).

Act III takes place on the day of the Mastersingers' contest. Walther comes to Sachs and sings a song; Sachs writes it down. Beckmesser steals Walther's song (thinking it belongs to Sachs) but performs it so badly (misreading Sachs's handwriting; his mistakes are textual as well as musical) that Walther gets his chance. He wins the contest, the girl, and membership in the guild. This last honor is by now a bittersweet one, but he accepts it in the name of German Art.

ACHTUNG! MOMENTS

Act I: The rousing overture that leads directly into the opening chorus, which is coming from church. Walther's song and ensemble "Am stillen Herd," which deteriorates into mayhem, with Beckmesser criticizing, Sachs defending, and the Mastersingers and onlookers commenting. This twenty-five-minute scene ends the act.

Act II: This hourlong act is nearly perfect, without an ounce of extra music: Sachs's philosophical, introspective monologue, "Was duftet doch der Flieder," is lovely and gentle; the finale,

The spear-carrying Brünnhilde atop her horse, flying through the air, carrying a dead hero to Valhalla. A candid shot.

beginning with the words "Jerum! Jerum!," includes Beckmess-er's serenade with Sach's snide commentary and is genuinely funny; the ensuing ensemble and fugal finale are a free-for-all that somehow manages to stay together brilliantly.

Act III: Sachs's musings on the world's madness, "Wahn! Wahn!"; the beautiful, optimistic quintet "Selig, wie die Sonne"; Walther's prize song "Morgenlich leuchtend im rosigen Schein"; the jubilant finale.

Der Ring des Nibelungen (The Ring of the Nibelung)

A prelude and three operas
First complete performance: Bayreuth, August 1876
Libretto: Written by the composer

To say that Wagner's *Der Ring des Nibelungen* is the grandest, most ambitious, most multifaceted work in the history of opera is not an overstatement. The idea began after the 1848 revolution with Wagner's fascination with the Hohenstaufen Emperor Fried-rich Barbarossa and took shape with his discovery of the Norse-Germanic epic *Das Nibelungenlied*. Wagner saw Barbarossa as the "rebirth" of the pagan Siegfried and felt that *Das Nibelungen-lied* offered enough space for him to set to music his image of society's ills and corruptions and its subsequent destruction and replacement by hope and love. At first he sketched a prose play about Barbarossa but mythologized him; Wagner's obsession with world domination, socialism, and power took in pagan and Christian ideas (he also thought about an opera on the life of Christ and one on Achilles), German and Greek myths. The Grail might as well have been the Nibelungen hoard of gold—it didn't matter: the ideas did. Eventually the Barbarossa idea went by the wayside and Wagner became completely embroiled in the Nibelung Saga.

The prose draft of *Siegfrieds Tod* (Siegfried's Death, eventually *Götterdämmerung*) was completed in October 1848, but the composer soon realized that the audience would need an explanation as to how Siegfried came to be murdered. He wrote the text to *Der Junge Siegfried*, which eventually became *Siegfried*, and then went further back and wrote *Die Walküre* as a lead-up to Siegfried's life, and then *Das Rheingold* as a prologue to the cycle of three operas. He began composing the music, in order, in 1853, but after the second act of *Siegfried*, in 1857, he stopped to write *Tristan und Isolde* and *Die Meistersinger von Nürnberg*. After picking them up again, he finally completed the four operas in 1874. Wagner hated the confined stage space and showy decor of the theater in Munich and further thought that being able to see the orchestra and conductor was a distraction, and he set about getting a theater built to his specifications. He chose the simple town of Bayreuth, since, as he put it, "there was no other reason for visiting" the place. But the first two operas were performed in 1869 and '70, respectively, in Munich to please his patron, King Ludwig II, who was tired of waiting, and it was not until 1876, when his theater in Bayreuth was completed, that the whole cycle was premiered.

Wagner was already legendary, and the first Ring Cycle was

attended by Franz Liszt, Kaiser Wilhelm I, King Ludwig II, Emperor Pedro II of Brazil, Anton Bruckner, Friedrich Nietzsche, Pyotr Tchaikovsky, and Camille Saint-Saëns. Tchaikovsky notoriously announced, when *Götterdämmerung* was over, that "it was like being freed from prison"; many felt the cycle was simply too long (fifteen hours is a long time, even if it is spread over four evenings, with a break between the third and fourth), with the critic of France's *Le Figaro* calling it "the dreams of a lunatic."

Of course, now all criticisms are moot—why bother? The fifteen-plus-hour allegory on human love, lust, power and its abuses, greed, fate, betrayal, suffering, class structure, and redemption has been appreciated on so many levels that it is universally acknowledged as the masterwork it is. One cannot avoid being bowled over by these operas, individually or as a complete cycle. The more one hears them, the more one hears *in* them. Wagner insisted that the music, as well as the text, tell the story; hence his creation of leitmotifs. These are melodic and harmonic snatches—sometimes just a three-note sequence, often longer—that stand for something or someone, and though they're consistent, they also change somewhat and grow throughout the cycle as the characters change and grow. There are leitmotifs associated with all the characters, with power, with Siegfried's sword, with the Ring itself, with the Curse, with the gods, and with the changes in stature and importance of all these things. There are nearly two hundred of them, and even the casual listener cannot avoid becoming subconsciously as well as consciously aware of them. In Wagner's musical world, they replace the static arias, duets, and finales so familiar in opera as focal points for the listener: the melodies, and there are plenty of them, are un-ending—they constantly transmogrify to further describe and clarify the action. You can pay attention to them or not—specific knowledge of them only enhances the experience.

Consisting of *Das Rheingold* (The Rhine Gold), *Die Walküre* (The Valkyrie), *Siegfried*, and *Götterdämmerung* (Twilight of the Gods), the Ring's story begins with the theft of the most power-ful gold conceivable. Whoever makes a ring of the stolen gold while, at the same time, renouncing love will become ruler of the world. That, as the late comedian Anna Russell, in her most famous comedic/musical monologue once said, is "the gimmick." Unfortunately for the characters, by the end of the story—that is, the final curtain of the fourth opera—there's nothing much left to rule. Fortunately for the audience, up to that point, there has been just about everything. Wagner's goal with the Ring Cycle was to create an epic work or series of works. He used the word "tetralogy," describing the operas as "stage festival play for three days and a preliminary evening." The cycle would realize his theory of *Gesamtkunstwerk*, a unity of words, music, and stage action designed to intermingle perfectly, each playing an equal role. And since Wagner considered himself a brilliant playwright, philosopher, stage director, and poet as well as composer, who better than he to concoct such perfection?

The Ring Cycle's music surpasses even Wagner's most fantas-tic megalomaniacal fantasies; never before or since have so many feelings been expressed so vividly and viscerally in one work. *Gesamtkunstwerk* or not, and twenty-eight years in the making, the Ring Cycle offers an amazing parable of humanity, replete with love, lust, loyalty, and the thirst for and corruption of power.

"Wagner has some wonderful moments," wrote a critic many years ago, "and some terrible half-hours." See if you agree.

Das Rheingold (The Rhine Gold)
Prologue and one act (four scenes)

WHO'S WHO

The Rhinemaidens (two sopranos and a mezzo-soprano)
Alberich, a Nibelung dwarf (baritone)
Mime, another Nibelung dwarf, Alberich's brother (tenor)
Wotan, chief of the gods (bass-baritone)
Fricka, Wotan's wife, goddess of marriage (mezzo-soprano)
Loge, god of fire (tenor)
Fasolt, a giant/castle builder (bass-baritone)
Fafner, a giant/castle builder (bass)
Freia, goddess of love, Fricka's sister (soprano)
Erda, earth goddess (contralto)
Donner, god of thunder (baritone)

WHAT'S HAPPENING

In and about the Rhine River, legendary time

The Rhinemaidens are guardians of the magical gold, but the dwarf Alberich steals the treasure and makes a ring, following the instructions to renounce love at the same time. He's all set to rule the world, but the god Wotan, along with Loge, the wily god of fire, travels to the Nibelheim, a land below the surface inhabited by dwarves (including Alberich's brother, Mime) and usurps the Ring, so Alberich puts a curse on it, promising it will wreak destruction upon whoever possesses it. Wotan decides to use the Ring to reclaim Freia, without whose golden apples the gods cannot remain immortal. (Wotan had previously traded Freia to Fasolt and Fafner for their construction of his castle, Valhalla, and they fell in love with her.) As soon as the giants are in possession of the Ring, Fafner kills Fasolt. Erda, the earth goddess, appears to Wotan and predicts the downfall of the gods. The curse has begun its work, even as the gods take up residency in the magnificent Valhalla.

ACHTUNG! MOMENTS

Das Rheingold is the least satisfying of the four Ring operas, particularly for the newcomer, but it is essential to have at least a slim familiarity with it in order to "get" the Ring Cycle. My advice is to play it through, figure out what's going on, and move on immediately to *Die Walküre*, considered by most to be the most human and lyrical of the group.

True to the concept of *Gesamtkunstwerk*, and because the purpose of *Das Rheingold* is to introduce the characters, basic plot, and themes, there aren't many highlights as such. Each scene of its one-act, two-and-a-half-hour length melds into the next; it is a seamless chain of events. Nevertheless, within the fabric of such a structure, there are a handful of spectacular moments.

Opening scene: Wagner's depiction of the Rhine River consists of a drone—the instruments, beginning very quietly, play an E flat for four minutes, undulating slightly: it sets the tone for the entire cycle. The sound is almost subliminal at first—it seems to have no beginning, as if the universe were being created. After the scene between Alberich and the Rhinemaidens in which he steals the gold, the second scene introduces us to Wotan and Fricka and the other characters. In Scene iii, Wotan and Loge's descent to and ascent from the Nibelheim to retrieve the gold is framed by orchestral interludes featuring a gaggle of eighteen tuned anvils that depict the work of the dwarves who are enslaved by the now-powerful Alberich. In the final scene Alberich's curse is potent and vicious and should be remembered; it returns frequently during the whole cycle as a reminder that evil and doom are always nearby. Erda's gloomy prediction to Wotan is a show-stopper, as is Donner's summoning of a thunderstorm to clear the air ("Heda! Heda! Hedo!") for the spectacular entry of the Gods into Valhalla.

Die Walküre (The Valkyrie)
Three acts

WHO'S WHO
   Wotan, chief of the gods (bass-baritone)
   Fricka, Wotan's wife, goddess of marriage (mezzo-soprano)
   Siegmund, the mortal son of Wotan (tenor)
   Sieglinde, the mortal daughter of Wotan, Siegmund's twin
      (soprano)
   Brünnhilde, the favorite Valkyrie daughter of Wotan and Erda
      (soprano)

Eight other Valkyries, daughters of Wotan and Erda (sopranos,
mezzo-sopranos, contraltos)
Hunding, Sieglinde's husband, the chief of the Neidungs (bass)

WHAT'S HAPPENING
In the middle of nowhere, legendary times

Sieglinde and Siegmund, mortal twins born to Wotan and separated soon thereafter, reunite as adults when a storm drives Siegmund to seek shelter in Sieglinde's hut. Sieglinde has been living there with Hunding, the man to whom she is unhappily married and who is also the enemy of Siegmund. The twins soon fall in love and flee together, taking with them the sword Nothung (yes, the sword has a name), once belonging to their father, which he had placed in a tree long before and which only a true hero could extract. Fricka, who guards the sanctity of marriage, is angry with Siegmund for stealing Sieglinde from Hunding, and she commands Wotan *not* to help Siegmund in the ensuing duel between the two men. Wotan orders Brünnhilde, his favorite among the nine Valkyries, not to side with Siegmund. Brünnhilde, sympathetic to her mortal siblings, crosses her father and promises victory to Siegmund. However, urged on by Fricka, Wotan appears, shatters the sword, and presides over his own son's death. Brünnhilde rescues the shattered pieces of Nothung; she also rescues Sieglinde, who is pregnant with Siegmund's child. Wotan must punish Brünnhilde for this act of disobedience, so he calls upon Loge to create a fire around a huge rock upon which she will sleep until she is rescued—a feat that can be achieved only by a great hero.

— *Weep, Shudder, Die* —

Wotan's Farewell to Brünnhilde: A tender embrace for his disobedient daughter just before he puts her to sleep on a rock surrounded by fire. You can't be too strict with these kids.

ACHTUNG! MOMENTS

If truth be known, there's very little in this opera that isn't a delight: the plot moves quickly by Wagnerian standards (in Act II, Wotan tells Brünnhilde the whole story of *Das Rheingold*, which we certainly didn't have to hear again—or did we?), and the leitmotifs—those little bits of melody that identify people, places, and things—have begun to become familiar enough that it doesn't seem so much of a jumble. *Die Walküre* is the most popular of the four operas; most consider it the easiest. Whatever that means.

Act I: The opening orchestral storm sequence, filled with anxiety and turmoil. All of Scene iii: Siegmund calls upon his father for help, and he spots the sword in the tree; Sieglinde describes how, after being abducted, as she was being married to Hunding, a stranger appeared and plunged the sword into the tree ("Der Männer Sippe") and how she believes that Siegmund will save her. The doors and windows of the house disappear, and Siegmund sings a rapturous aria to the arrival of spring and new love ("Winterstürme"). He pulls the sword from the tree in an orgasmic eruption. Revelation upon revelation; the twins, now in love, race off into the night.

Act II: Brünnhilde's battle cry, "Hojotoho!," a much-parodied but thrilling two-minute yelp that defines a Wagnerian soprano's strength and ease with high notes; the beautiful "announcement of death" scene in which Brünnhilde tells Siegmund that he will die in battle.

Act III: The thrilling, much-imitated and -borrowed (as in *Apocalypse Now*) "Ride of the Valkyries"; Wotan's raging at Brünnhilde; their moving duet; "Wotan's Farewell"; the "Magic Fire Music."

Siegfried
Three acts

WHO'S WHO

Siegfried, the son of Siegmund and Sieglinde (tenor)
Mime, Alberich's brother, acting as father to Siegfried (tenor)
Alberich (bass-baritone)
Forest Bird (soprano)
Brünnhilde, the favorite daughter of Wotan and Erda (soprano)
Fafner, a giant/castle builder, now turned into a dragon (bass)
The Wanderer (Wotan in disguise; bass-baritone)
Erda, goddess of earth (contralto)

WHAT'S HAPPENING

In the middle of nowhere, legendary times

Sieglinde has died giving birth to her brother's child, Siegfried, who was found and raised by Mime (remember *Das Rheingold*?). Siegfried, now a man, seeks to reclaim the Ring by slaying Fafner (remember *Das Rheingold*?), who lives in a cave nearby, having taken on the form of a dragon. The Wanderer enters, and he and Mime question each other. Upon Siegfried's return, Mime explains that only one who knows no fear can reforge the shards of the sword that Sieglinde had with her when she died. That man is Siegfried. Siegfried succeeds in reforging Nothung (the sword with a name). Siegfried kills Fafner and takes the Ring. He tastes some of the dragon's blood, thus gaining the ability to understand the instructions of the Forest Bird as well as the evil intentions of Mime, who wants to kill Siegfried and take the gold. (This is no time to be questioning what does and does not make sense.) Siegfried kills Mime; we hear Alberich laughing from a distance. The Forest Bird's chirpings lead him toward the spot where Brünnhilde lies inside her circle of fire. Wotan tries to stop him, but Siegfried, stupid, insensitive, and uninterested, cannot figure out that the Wanderer is his grandfather and he breaks Wotan's spear. By so doing, rulership passes from god to man. Siegfried then finds Brünnhilde, who is at first horrified at the thought of surrender—she has gone to sleep a goddess and awakened as a woman. But she can't resist the forces of love.

ACHTUNG! MOMENTS

Many people consider *Siegfried* the Ring Cycle's bore, but it is, rather, a weird sort of scherzo—a series of duets, many of them quite funny in a grotesque sort of way. Act I: Mime/Siegfried, Mime/Wanderer, Mime/Siegfried. Act II: Wanderer/Alberich, Mime/Siegfried, Siegfried/Fafner (dragon), Siegfried/Mime. Act III: Wanderer/Erda, Wanderer/Siegfried, Siegfried/Brünnhilde. The third act, composed after a hiatus of several years (to compose *Tristan und Isolde* and *Die Meistersinger von Nürnberg*), contains one overwhelming scene after another, culminating in the scene of Siegfried's discovery of the fire and Brünnhilde, her awakening, their first kiss, her acknowledging love and his acknowledging fear, and their mutual rapture. Each eighty-minute (!) act should be approached as broken into fifteen- to twenty-five-minute scenes; they are less daunting that way.

Act I: Siegfried's forging song "Nothung! Nothung!," the most challenging scene for tenor ever composed.

Act II: "Forest Murmurs," wherein Siegfried sits back and listens to the sounds of the forest before he blows his horn and awakens the dragon; the Siegfried-dragon fight; the scene in which Siegfried can read the mind of the evil Mime, who wants to kill him.

Act III: The orchestral prelude; the Wanderer's confrontation with Erda; Brünnhilde's awakening; the lengthy final duet, "Heil dir, Sonne!"

Götterdämmerung (Twilight of the Gods)
Prologue and three acts

WHO'S WHO

In addition to some of the characters already introduced:

Gunther, king of the Gibichungs (baritone)

Gutrune, Gunther's unmarried sister (soprano)

Hagen, their half brother (bass)

Waltraute, Brünnhilde's sister (mezzo-soprano)

Three Norns, Erda's daughters (soprano, mezzo-soprano, contralto)

WHAT'S HAPPENING

In the middle of nowhere, legendary times

In the Prologue, Erda's gloomy daughters, the Norns, weave the rope of destiny. Siegfried gives the Ring to Brünnhilde, and they part as Siegfried travels down the Rhine on new adventures.

In Act I, he comes upon the Gibichungs, a race of people who live near the river. Hagen, the son of Alberich, wants to recapture the Ring. He plots with Gunther and Gutrune, and they give Siegfried a drug that destroys his memory, making him think he loves Gutrune and that he must deliver Brünnhilde (and the Ring) to Gunther. In disguise, and still duped by the drug, Siegfried takes the Ring from Brünnhilde, places it on his own finger, and allows her to think he loves another woman.

In Act II, Siegfried takes Brünnhilde back to the Gibichung Hall, where she is to marry Gunther, but Brünnhilde flies into a rage, misunderstanding what is going on. She swears to help Hagen and Gunther kill Siegfried by telling them where his weak spot lies.

In Act III, after a strange meeting between Siegfried and the Rhinemaidens (remember *Das Rheingold?*), Siegfried, out hunting with the Gibichungs, is given a draft that suddenly makes him remember everything. Hagen kills Siegfried, but when they return to the Gibichung Hall and he tries to take the Ring from Siegfried, Brünnhilde appears and stops him. Having discovered, too late, that Siegfried was not responsible for his actions, she orders a huge funeral pyre and joins Siegfried in death. The sorrow, love, and despair of Brünnhilde's sacrifice create a mael-strom: the Rhine overflows; the hall collapses; the Rhinemaid-ens appear, drag Hagen to his death, and reclaim the Ring, now cleansed of its curse. The funeral fire spreads to Valhalla. The power of the gods has ended.

ACHTUNG! MOMENTS

Like the rest of the Ring Cycle—only more so—*Götterdämmer-ung* is a fiesta of continuous music, and therefore it is difficult to pinpoint its truly superb moments; in fact, given its outlandish length (four and a half hours), it has very few dead spots. It is the culmination of the Grand Saga and, as such, is action-packed and shows Wagner at his least tedious.

Prologue: Siegfried and Brünnhilde's duet: an ecstatic love fest, filled with energy, blazing high notes, and great volume. Siegfried's Rhine journey: a brilliant orchestral depiction of Sieg-fried's trip down the Rhine, complete with rolling waves, sun glistening on water, calm, and smooth sailing—one of the great instrumental depictions in opera. Crank up the volume.

Act I: The "blood brotherhood" oath, in which the drugged, duped Siegfried swears blood allegiance to Gunther. Hagen's watch: left alone, the evil Hagen wallows in the fact that his "bet-ters" have been tricked into bringing him the Ring. Siegfried's ar-rival on the rock disguised as Gunther and Brünnhilde's horror: a few minutes of real horror and brutality.

Act II: The entire act is riveting, from the hypnotic, hallu-cinatory opening scene in which Alberich comes to Hagen in a dream; Hagen's rousing summoning of his vassals; the wedding march; and from the moment Brünnhilde recognizes Siegfried and flies into a rage through the end of the sixty-five-minute act. Great theater and great music.

Act III: Siegfried's monologue before his death, in which he recalls Brünnhilde; the ceremonial funeral music; Brünnhilde's immolation scene. This last piece—seventeen minutes long, with its orchestral epilogue—truly is the musical and dramatic peak of the cycle: many of the leitmotifs meet here, leitmotifs that by now you know and recognize (even if you don't know their associations, you will be familiar with the melodies). By the time it's over, the listener is not only mesmerized, he or she has a sense of completion and satisfaction that comes with no other Western piece of music, art, or literature I can think of.

Mozart's Operas

NO COMPARISONS POSSIBLE

Wolfgang Amadeus Mozart (1756–1791) remains uncategorizable. We all know he was born in Salzburg, Austria, and by the age of five was the world's most famous and infamous child prodigy, traveling from palace to palace with his father, Leopold, and sister, Nannerl (whom he called, with great affection, "Horse Face"). It seems equally ridiculous to attempt to sum up Mozart's career in a few simple sentences. Suffice it to say he wrote better, and more, music than anyone before or since. And then there's Peter Shaffer's play/movie *Amadeus*, which, with its half-truths and fine music, makes us think we actually know this unique character, who enjoyed gambling and practical jokes as much as composing his twenty-seven piano concertos, forty symphonies, and dozens upon dozens of other works.

But what of Mozart as an opera composer? You'll notice that he gets his own category, since both his Italian operas and his

German operas are more Mozartian than of any nationality—he was a musical sponge, picking up styles from whatever city he was visiting as a child, and his style is—well, Mozartian. His operas are fat-free; never will you find moments that emptily set the scene; everything moves the action along, and, yes, every note is interesting. Though some operas by even the greatest composers—Verdi, Puccini, Wagner—can afford to be cut a bit here and there, Mozart's operas are so perfect that each note counts.

What makes us so love *Figaro*, *Così Fan Tutte*, *Don Giovanni*, and *The Magic Flute* is what makes us love all great works: they are beautiful and timeless, funny and profound, sublime and ridiculous. *Don Giovanni*, to take one example, can be presented as a comedic piece (look at all those women, crying over the great Lothario while he mocks them) or the dramatic story of a truly evil man rightly consigned to Hell (he rapes and murders—not so funny). Or recall *The Magic Flute*. It, too, can be read as a mysterious Masonic parable, as a grand romp through a very bizarre fairyland, or just as totally singable entertainment. Or all three. This may be the key to Mozart's brilliance and continuing popularity: like Shakespeare's, like Picasso's, his work is infinitely variable and interpretable—and always unmistakably . . . er . . . Mozartian.

Le Nozze di Figaro (The Marriage of Figaro)
Four acts
First performance: Burgtheater, Vienna, 1786
Libretto: Lorenzo Da Ponte

Le Nozze di Figaro originated as a play by Pierre Beaumarchais, a French writer and protorevolutionary. In *Figaro*, he presented the public with a not-very-happily-married count and countess and a servant smarter and more moral than his masters—in other words, highly critical of the existing social order. Performances of the play were banned in Austria, but it was published, and Mozart (a fan of titillation of all sorts) was intrigued. He and his librettist, Lorenzo Da Ponte, worked quickly and furtively on the piece (Mozart's letters contain very little information about the opera's composition), with Da Ponte toning down many of the original references to French politics but keeping the sexual shenanigans in place. Mozart's musical characterizations tell us everything we have to know about love, honor, and justice. The result was a resounding success. By the third performance, the emperor banned encores for fear that *Figaro* would go on through the night.

WHO'S WHO

Figaro, Count Almaviva's servant (bass)

Susanna, Countess Almaviva's maid (soprano)

Count Almaviva (baritone)

Countess Rosina Almaviva (soprano)

Cherubino, Countess Almaviva's page (male role played by mezzo-soprano or soprano)

Dr. Bartolo (bass)

Marcellina, the count's ex-housekeeper (mezzo-soprano)

WHAT'S HAPPENING
Near Seville, 1780s

A count and a countess carry on a quixotic relationship with each other and their servants. There are plotting and subplotting galore, most of which are aimed at the roguish count.

Act I dawns on the wedding day of Figaro and Susanna. The count, lusting after Susanna, wishes he could share in the nuptial delights (the feudal *droit de seigneur* allowed a nobleman to sleep with his female servants before their weddings); Marcellina, a somewhat older woman yearning for Figaro, wishes he were marrying her (and he will have to, if he fails to repay the money he has borrowed from Dr. Bartolo). The just-teenage Cherubino, a page, who desires most of the women, is found hiding in the countess's bedroom.

In Act II, we see first how the count's infidelity is saddening the wise countess, but the romantic antics continue and are confounded by much hiding, peeping, and uncovering.

In Act III, the count overhears the others plotting and gets more and more irate. We also discover that Dr. Bartolo and Marcellina are the father and mother of Figaro, which, needless to say, immediately gets Figaro out of debt. They might as well get married, along with their son and Susanna.

In Act IV, Susanna is still determined to foil the count. She leads him to a rendezvous—where he meets up with his wife instead (leading to some of the most beautiful vocal music ever written). By the final curtain, all is forgiven.

AH, MOZART

Act I: Figaro's arias "Se vuol ballare" and "Non più andrai." In the first aria Figaro expresses his anger with the class system he finds himself in, sarcastically addressing his aria to the absent count. In the second, he teases Cherubino mercilessly as the young man is sent off to join the army. In these two arias, we learn quickly what Figaro is all about—his wit, charm, and dissatisfaction.

Act II: The countess's aria "Porgi amor": here we meet the countess for the first time, and alone, she reflects on the count's infidelity with great yearning. A sad, brief, dignified, and lovely aria, utterly devoid of self-pity; the music, even more than the words, tells the story. Cherubino's arietta "Voi che sapete," in which, forlorn, he says that he feels genuine love and that Susanna and the countess can relate to what he feels. The finale, "Esci, omai, garzon malnato": this is the most stupendously constructed finale to any act in opera. It begins as a duet, then becomes a trio, then a quartet, and so on, each time changing tempo, and for twenty minutes gets more and more complicated and funnier and funnier. For sheer forward propulsion and wit, it has never been equaled.

Act III: The count's recitative and aria "Hai già vinto la causa!," a vicious monologue in which the count realizes that he's being duped and vows revenge; the sextet "Riconosci in questo amplesso," a wildly funny piece in which the revelations of Figaro's background are dealt with; the aria "Dove sono," a stunning piece of reflection in which the countess first wonders sadly where all the happy days have gone but then begins to think positively, a showpiece that is both lovely and touching.

Act IV: Figaro's aria "Aprite un po' quegli occhi" (Open your eyes a little), his advice to men (this is when he thinks Susanna is about to be unfaithful to him with the count); Susanna, knowing Figaro is surreptitiously watching her, singing "Deh, vieni, non tardar," a tender love song of anticipation; and the opera's final moments, after everyone has figured out who is fooling whom, the count asks the countess's forgiveness in what is arguably all of opera's most beautiful phrase, which is followed by a merry free-for-all.

Don Giovanni

Two acts
First performance: Theatre of the Estates, Prague, 1787
Libretto: Lorenzo Da Ponte

Don Giovanni is the portrait of a man you love to hate. Based on the legendary character of Don Juan Tenorio, Mozart and Da Ponte's Giovanni is sometimes scandalous, sometimes endearing, but always maddening. He leaves a trail of heartbroken women and their cuckolded men, but he laughs everything off and strikes again. Refusing to reform or repent, Giovanni dies to uphold his motto: long live liberty, long live women, long live wine, long live the strength and glory of mankind. But the great thing about Mozart and Da Ponte's take on the story is that the opera's music and text are somewhat more complicated: the don can be seen as a truly oversexed, amoral hell-raiser, a randy young guy who is merely having a good time, or a boastful creep; he does not consummate any sexual act during the opera—it's all hearsay, flirting, and bluster. Maybe. And more: Does Donna Anna have the hots for Don Giovanni? Is she pretending to be outraged because her betrothed, Don Ottavio, is a drip? Is Donna Elvira crazy—or pregnant? Is Leporello, Giovanni's servant, horrified by or entertained by his master? Discuss.

In other words, is *Don Giovanni* a *dramma giocoso* (playful drama), as it is designated in both score and libretto, or *opera buffa* (comic opera) as Mozart referred to it in his own catalog? It is designed to be both. The overture, for example, begins in a dark, minor mode and proceeds into lighthearted, witty merriment. At the opera's end, the double finale provides further proof. The first part shows the corrupt, immoral don dragged to Hell for refusing to repent; its second part consists of an upbeat sextet in which the other characters decide what they will do with the rest of their lives. In the nineteenth century, moralistic audiences preferred that the second part of the finale be omitted, making the opera far more *dramma* than *giocoso* or *buffa* and thereby doing Mozart a disservice. He wanted a fusion of tragic and comic, darkness and light, and he achieved it from beginning to end as no other composer could. Each major character except for Don Giovanni gets two arias; arias are mostly moments of introspection or deep feeling, and Mozart was clearly interested in keeping us at a distance from the don so the interpretation could be either *dramma* or *giocoso*. He does, actually, have two solos: one is a drinking song, seventy seconds long; the other is a serenade, which he sings when disguised as Leporello. He's endlessly fascinating, but who is he?

There is enough stupendous music—arias, duets, trios, quartets, ensembles—in this one opera to fill three, and there is no sense of padding in its two-hour-and-forty-five-minute span. The result is what is often considered the greatest opera ever written.

WHO'S WHO

Don Giovanni, a young nobleman (baritone)
Leporello, Giovanni's servant (bass or baritone)
The Commendatore (bass)
Donna Anna, the Commendatore's daughter (soprano)
Don Ottavio, Donna Anna's betrothed (tenor)
Donna Elvira, a lady of Burgos (soprano)
Zerlina, a country maiden (soprano or mezzo-soprano)
Masetto, Zerlina's betrothed (baritone)

WHAT'S HAPPENING

Seville, Spain, seventeenth century

In Act I, we first encounter Leporello, who is waiting for his master, Don Giovanni, who soon makes a hurried exit from the house of Donna Anna, his most recent amorous target. After the don wins a fatal duel (with Anna's father, the Commendatore), insults a former amour (Donna Elvira), and schemes to seduce a young peasant bride-to-be (Zerlina), the injured parties join forces to bring the scoundrel down.

However, in Act II, Don Giovanni unintentionally beats them to it, flippantly issuing a dinner invitation to the memorial statue of the dead Commendatore. When the statue arrives for the banquet, he challenges his host: "Think upon your sins and repent." The don answers with an emphatic *"No!"* even as he is dragged into the flames of Hell.

AH, MOZART

With all the stunning numbers in this opera, it's not easy to choose high points. Just to give you an idea of the craft and joys to behold here, hear this: After the dark/light overture, Leporello sings an aria explaining his exhaustion and displeasure at working for the don, but it's playful and upbeat; he's clearly a coconspirator in some way. Immediately, and with a pickup in tempo, the don is seen being chased by Donna Anna, whom he has allegedly attempted to rape, and they sing at the same time, but with totally different rhythms and at odds with each other. As she runs off, her father, the Commendatore, appears, and he and the don duel. The don runs him through, and as he dies, the three bass-baritone voices—the don's, the Commendatore's, and Leporello's—sing a slow trio, each expressing his own feelings, the dark voices intertwining but never meeting. Immediately thereafter, Donna Anna returns, horrified, with her betrothed, Don Ottavio, and they react to the death of the Commendatore in another duet. We have met and seen five characters in action, watched the result of an attempted rape, and seen a murder: including the overture, this has taken seventeen minutes.

Act I: The first seventeen minutes of the opera, described above; Leporello's catalog aria, in which he takes great joy in describing to the half-crazy Donna Elvira all of the don's other conquests; the duet of seduction "Là ci darem la mano" between

Don Giovanni and Zerlina (note how he speeds up near the end, putting on the pressure, when he thinks that she may be chickening out); the quartet "Non ti fidar, o misera," in which Elvira tries to convince Anna and Ottavio that Giovanni is not to be trusted while he tries to convince them that Elvira is insane; Donna Anna's "Or sai chi l'onore," in which she demands revenge against the don, whom she has just recognized. Note the recitative between her and Ottavio before the aria beginning with the words "Don Ottavio, son morta!" Doesn't it sound as if he is getting off on her description of the almost rape? Don Ottavio's "Dalla sua pace," a meltingly beautiful aria in which he sings of his devotion to Donna Anna's happiness. Because Ottavio seems to be such an enigmatic, weak character, Mozart gave him two of the most beautiful tenor arias he ever composed so that the audience would have to be interested in him.

Act II: The don's sexy, insincere serenade "Deh, vieni alla finestra"; the sextet "Solo, solo in buio loco"; Don Ottavio's showpiece aria (note the very long phrases, requiring a solid line and breath control), "Il mio tesoro," in which he promises to avenge Donna Anna; Donna Elvira's recitative and aria "In quali eccessi," a mini–mad scene in which she lets all of her drama-queen behavior hang out; "Non mi dir," Donna Anna's announcement to Ottavio that she wishes to put off their wedding until Heaven is kinder to her—a dramatic statement which starts out sorrowfully and ends in a blaze of coloratura. And of course, the supper scene and epilogue—the double finale.

Così Fan Tutte (They're All the Same)

Two acts
First performance: Burgtheater, Vienna, 1790
Libretto: Lorenzo Da Ponte

The emperor himself, Joseph II, suggested the subject matter of *Così Fan Tutte*, which was said to be based on an incident that had occurred in Vienna a few months before. Two engaged men are complacent about the faithfulness of their fiancées; the cynical Don Alfonso feels the need to set them straight. The don's theory is that all women have a common problem: they cannot be trusted and, therefore, must be tested. Do you think this will turn out well?

Mozart found Da Ponte's libretto about faithless lovers "frivolous and degrading." In August 1879, while Mozart was hard at work on *Così*, he wrote to his wife, Constanze, who was in Baden taking the waters (and apparently a bit more), "I do wish that you would sometimes not make yourself so cheap. . . . Remember that you yourself once admitted to me that you were inclined to comply too easily." Could he have been taking the situation in the opera personally? Whatever the case, the music and understanding of human fallibility transcend any personal dissatisfactions. As always, Mozart saw all sides of a story, and he created a work at once satirical and loving, bitter and forgiving. But questions remain: Do the couples return to their original alliances, or do they stay together as they have found themselves in the opera? Are there any winners?

WHO'S WHO

Fiordiligi (soprano)

Dorabella, Fiordiligi's sister (soprano or mezzo-soprano)

Despina, their maid (soprano)

Ferrando, Dorabella's fiancé (tenor)

Guglielmo, Fiordiligi's fiancé (baritone)

Don Alfonso, elderly philosopher (bass)

WHAT'S HAPPENING

Naples, eighteenth century

In Act I, Don Alfonso's plan goes into action: Ferrando and Guglielmo will pretend to leave for war; in fact, they will reappear in disguise as two Albanians. Don Alfonso recommends the young men to the ladies, aided by the maid Despina, who thinks her mistresses should look for amusement while their lovers are away. At first, the fiancées successfully fend off the Albanians' attentions.

In Act II, they finally weaken, with Dorabella falling first, followed with far more reluctance by Fiordiligi. Just as a double wedding is in the offing, the bridegrooms enter. They are now Ferrando and Guglielmo again, carrying their Albanian disguises. The women plead for mercy, and the men grant it, with everyone praising tolerance and agreeing that reason must rule.

AH, MOZART

Although there are at least a half-dozen superb arias in *Così Fan Tutte*, this really is an opera of ensembles. The opening scene, a three-part trio for the men, lets us know in eight minutes what we're dealing with: two foolish, boastful young men and a wiser, perhaps bitter older man; the next five minutes introduce us to the sisters pining in duet over their men with great drama; then Alfonso enters and tells the sisters, in a trio, that their loves must go to the army and the drama-queen level rises—and rises and rises. Mozart knew how to mingle voices and emotions as no other composer. I'll just list the particularly juicy musical moments—*Così*, like its two sister operas discussed above, tends to be an unbroken chain of musical delights—and very intuitive portraits of the characters.

Act I: The quintet "Sento oh Dio"; the trio "Soave sia il vento" (the most famous—and tender—piece in the opera, seemingly one of the few oases of genuine, rather than overhyped, feeling); Fiordiligi's aria "Come scoglio" (a parody of hand-to-forehead, hand-to-heart, "serious" arias, with wide, overly dramatic leaps and wild coloratura); Ferrando's aria "Una aura amorosa" (the last sincere outpouring of love and emotion in the opera—and it's in the first act).

Act II: The Ferrando-Guglielmo duet with chorus "Secondate, aurette amiche," a wonderful scene setting for seduction; Guglielmo and Dorabella's duet "Il cor vi dono" and Ferrando and Fiordiligi's duet "Fra gli amplessi" in which each man finally succeeds in turning the head of the other's fiancée; the problem remains: is this a good thing or a bad thing? And maybe Mozart wanted it that way, since tenor and soprano are usually paired off in opera? And the whole finale to the opera—the mock wedding in which we see how miserable Guglielmo is, the return of the two "original" fiancés, the denouement, and, perhaps, the end of the confusion. "How happy is the man who looks on the bright side of everything / And in all circumstances and trials lets himself be guided by reason," everyone sings. Mmmmmmmm.

Die Zauberflöte (The Magic Flute)

Two acts
First performance: Theater auf der Wieden, Vienna, 1791
Libretto: Emanuel Schikaneder

Here is an opera that at one level is an esoteric allegory of Freemasonry, at another, a fairy tale. At the same time, *Die Zauberflöte* is great entertainment, filled with characters and situations that are both believable and unbelievable. George Bernard Shaw wrote that the music of the high priest Sarastro "would not be out of place in the mouth of God." But then the bird catcher Papageno's melodies are practically folksy. The answer to these possible contradictions can be summed up in one word: Mozart. What other composer, in the entire history of classical music, is routinely capable of such contrasts of sound and mood, from noble to playful to sublime—sometimes all in the same scene?

Flute is replete with traditional fairy-tale elements (magical instruments, wicked queen versus noble "wizard," ordeals by fire and water, everything happening by threes) intermingling with symbols important to the Masonic movement, of which both Mozart and Schikaneder were members. The characters are thinly disguised figures of the times (including the anti-

Masonic Empress Maria Theresa as the Queen of the Night), and the piece's theme celebrates the triumph of courage, virtue, and wisdom, key requisites of the Masonic "brotherhood of man." If the truth be known, the Masonic stuff is too esoteric and misogynistic and there's too much mysticism that proves little. The music is sublime, but the opera has its longueurs (too much dialogue), and its overall effect is not as overwhelming as those of the three operas outlined above. Just my opinion, but I'm right.

Papageno finally meets Papagena, an arrangement clearly made on WeirdDate.com.

—— *Mozart's Operas* ——

WHO'S WHO

Tamino, an Egyptian prince (tenor)
The Queen of the Night (soprano)
Three ladies, the Queen of the Night's attendants (two sopranos and a mezzo-soprano)
Pamina, the Queen of the Night's daughter (soprano)
Papageno, a bird catcher (baritone)
Sarastro, high priest of Isis and Osiris (bass)
Papagena, a female bird catcher (soprano)

WHAT'S HAPPENING

Egypt, legendary time

In Act I, Prince Tamino enters, chased by a serpent; he faints before it can do him any damage. His rescuers are the three ladies of the Queen of the Night. They show him a picture of Pamina, the queen's daughter, who can be his if he will rescue her from the supposedly evil Sarastro. Accompanied by the clownish Papageno, Tamino begins his quest. He finds not only Pamina but the truth as well: that Sarastro is the force of good and the queen—consumed with hate—is really the villain of the piece.

In Act II, with Pamina as his guide, Tamino survives his trials, and both become initiates into Sarastro's noble order. Even Papageno triumphs, ending up with Papagena, the feathered female of his dreams. Not so lucky is the Queen of the Night: she and her dark ladies are banished by a sudden flood of the purest and noblest light.

AH, MOZART

Act I: The bird catcher Papageno's entrance aria; Tamino's lovely "Bildnis" aria as he gazes at a portrait of Pamina; the queen's aria "O zittre nicht" in which she tries to manipulate Tamino into finding and kidnapping her daughter, with its wild, endless vocal runs and showy leaps; the quintet in which the three ladies punish Papageno for lying (they place a lock on his lips, so he has to hum his lines).

Act II: Sarastro's prayer "O Isis und Osiris"; the Queen of the Night's vengeance aria "Der Hölle Rache" with its insanely high staccato notes (F above high C—stratospheric); Sarastro's noble "In diesen heil'gen Hallen"; Pamina's sad "Ach ich fühl's" (possibly the most beautiful aria Mozart ever wrote for soprano); Papageno's delicious duet with his Papagena.

Opera in English

IF YOU THINK IT'S EASIER TO UNDERSTAND, THINK AGAIN

Opera in English had a particularly poky start. It began with dialogue set to the music of pop tunes of the day in seventeenth-century England. John Blow, a so-so composer, wrote *Venus and Adonis* around 1683, but the first English masterpiece was definitely *Dido and Aeneas* by Henry Purcell, who died too young to compose any other full-length works (and *Dido* is only an hour long). Thomas Arne's *Thomas and Sally* was the first English opera to be sung in its entirety, but along with those of the later John Frederick Lampe and Michael William Balfe, Arne's operas used Italian opera as their models—they just happened to be in English. Gilbert and Sullivan, of course, wrote operas, but they were light, satiric, and of a different hue from what we are referring to as "opera." Not until the twentieth century, with

Benjamin Britten's *Peter Grimes* (1945), did British opera find a true voice. A major contemporary British composer is Thomas Adès, whose *Powder Her Face* and *The Tempest* have made quite a stir.

In addition, George Gershwin's *Porgy and Bess*, which began life on Broadway in 1935 and contains such American idioms as blues and jazz, is now considered a masterpiece, having gained "operatic" status only in 1976, when the Houston Grand Opera performed it as it was originally conceived, all three hours of it. Gian Carlo Menotti's *Amahl and the Night Visitors* and *The Consul* are American operas shot through with decidedly Italian influences. Douglas Moore's *The Ballad of Baby Doe* and Carlisle Floyd's *Susannah* contain folk elements; both are stageworthy and, like the others mentioned above, are heavily influenced by European forms: arias, duets, ensembles. Leonard Bernstein's *Trouble in Tahiti* and *A Quiet Place* are the only two of his stage works that he considered operas; the others, such as *West Side Story* and *Candide*, had one foot on Broadway. More recently, Philip Glass and John Adams have come to great fame as composers of both orchestral and stage music. Both are "minimalist" composers: their music relies on a steady pulse, consonant harmonies, repetition of musical phrases, or tiny figures with small and rhythmic or harmonic alterations. It isn't as boring as it sounds, but musical development is normally slower and more subtle in their works than in previous compositional methods. The music is easy to take and might sound simple, but it is not; it may seem utterly predictable, but it isn't. *Einstein on the Beach*, *Akhnaten*, and *Satyagraha* are a trilogy by Glass: each concerns a historic figure (Albert Einstein; Akhnaten, the first monotheistic pharaoh; and Mahatma Gandhi), who changed the world through nonviolent means, but each is more or less plotless. The five-hour, intermissionless *Einstein* was first performed in 1976; the audience was allowed to come and go as it pleased. John Adams's *Nixon in China* tells of the president's historic visit to that country and delves deeply into the players' characters: Henry Kissinger does not come out smelling like a rose. The subject and/or treatment may seem frivolous, but it is nothing of the sort. Adams's latest grand opera is the 2005 *Doctor Atomic*, about the testing of the first atomic bomb and its effect on its creators.

Other American composers to listen for are Mark Adamo (*Little Women*, *Lysistrata*), John Corigliano (*The Ghosts of Versailles*), Robert Moran (*The Juniper Tree*, *The Desert of Roses*), William Bolcom (*A View from the Bridge*), Tobias Picker (*An American Tragedy*), and Jake Heggie (*Dead Man Walking*). These "new" composers require a book unto themselves.

And not to put too fine a point on it, if you think you'd be better off listening to an opera in your native language, think again: The soprano voice in particular makes mincemeat of comprehension of the text. Invariably, even if the opera is in English and being sung to an English-speaking audience, the opera house supplies readable titles.

Henry Purcell

There are those who would argue that despite the intervening three hundred–plus years, Henry Purcell (1659–1695) is still the greatest British composer. During his brief life he composed more than twenty sonatas for violins, bass viol, and continuo, more than fifty songs, dozens upon dozens of anthems, a good deal of religious music and music for royal occasions, incidental music for forty-plus plays, fantasias for viols, odes and welcome songs, five semioperas (essentially plays with songs, choruses, and dances), and one sole opera: *Dido and Aeneas.* He was the organist at Westminster Abbey and a singer as well—probably singing both baritone and countertenor parts! Everything he wrote, in all forms, was masterly, and he was particularly noted for his sensitivity to text in his songs and theatrical settings. Purcell died just after his thirty-sixth birthday, and though the exact cause is not known, it was either tuberculosis or a chill caught one evening when he returned late from the theater to find that his wife had locked him out of the house. His early death was a catastrophe for British music (and opera); the other great English Baroque composer who comes to mind was George Frideric Handel—but he was a German who took up residence in London and composed operas to Italian texts. A side note: Pete Townshend of the rock band the Who has cited Purcell's harmonies as influencing many of the band's songs, with "Won't Get Fooled Again" a particularly strong example. I've never noticed.

Dido and Aeneas

Prologue and three acts

First performance: Josias Priest's Boarding School, London, 1689

Libretto: Nahum Tate

The music for the Prologue (and a couple of other scenes) has been lost, and, in fact, the only "pure" starting place for *Dido and Aeneas* is a libretto from the seventeenth century—probably from the original production. Composed in 1689 for a girls' boarding school, the earliest extant score comes from a copy made in 1750; it does not follow the same act divisions as the libretto. The opera takes the audiences through the pains of love and betrayal, introduces us to a sorceress, witches, courtiers, Cupids, and sailors, and moves from court to a witches' cave, then to a grove during a hunt, to a harbor, and to Dido's palace. The entire opera is only an hour long, and it is invariably performed in one act. The action is telescoped; it is a miniature masterpiece, short but epic. Some believe that the entire opera was meant as metaphor: Aeneas is King James II, led astray by the Sorceress, a symbol of Roman Catholicism; Dido is a representation of the British people, liable to be betrayed by the Papacy. Now that we know that, we can forget it and be deeply moved by Dido's plight.

WHO'S WHO

Dido, Queen of Carthage (soprano or mezzo-soprano)
Aeneas, Trojan prince (baritone)

Belinda, Dido's sister and handmaiden (soprano)
Sorceress (mezzo-soprano or countertenor)
A Sailor (tenor)

WHAT'S HAPPENING

Act I: Belinda and a second woman urge the unhappy Dido to consider marriage with the visiting Trojan prince, Aeneas. He enters, and at first she demurs, but she soon falls in love and agrees.

Act II: The Sorceress arranges for her elf, in the guise of the god-messenger Mercury, to convince Aeneas to leave Dido in order to found Rome, which would certainly make the queen die of grief. The witches rejoice and plan a thunderstorm to disturb the hunt the couple and their retinue are in the midst of. In the second scene, in a grove, Dido, Aeneas, Belinda, and others are rejoicing and enjoying nature. Thunder is heard, and Belinda sends the servants et al. back to the palace. Aeneas is left behind for a moment and is approached by the false Mercury, who tells him that Jove demands that he leave Carthage at once to found Rome. Torn but obedient, Aeneas agrees.

Act III: At the harbor, sailors sing a cynical song about love and fidelity, preparing to leave. The Sorceress and witches appear, pleased with the fact that their plan is working. Back at the palace, Dido and Belinda worry over Aeneas's absence. He appears, and the women are filled with foreboding, which is soon substantiated. Dido is appalled, and though Aeneas claims he will defy the gods and stay, she orders him to leave. Once he's gone, she prepares for her own death: "Death must come when he is gone." After singing a lament, she dies.

Act I: Dido's "Ah, Belinda," in which we really get a good picture of the lonely queen.

Act II: The Sorceress's incantation—over the top and self-consciously creepy and campy; the merry chorus in the grove—so delightfully Baroque.

Act III: The Sailor's snide, jolly song and dance. The final scene, known as "Dido's Lament" ("When I am laid in earth") is one of the most moving—yet simple—arias in all of opera. The accompaniment is a bass line repeated eleven times, while the sung text carries a melody. Note the sad plea of "Remember me"; it is set to music so beautiful and with such pathos that we will, indeed, remember Dido.

Benjamin Britten

Benjamin Britten (1913–1976) is, hands down, the most important and finest British composer since Henry Purcell, who died in 1695. Britten composed nearly one hundred works, including a dozen operas and three operalike church parables. *Peter Grimes*, his second opera, changed the face of British opera forever. The opera's themes are the cruel manner in which outsiders are treated in society (Britten was a homosexual and a conscientious objector), the fragility of innocence, and the ways in which power exploits. (These themes run through many of his operas, including *The Turn of the Screw* and *Death in Venice*.) His music is not always easy; although tunes are abundant, the musical idiom in which he works, though rarely atonal, takes some getting used to. The fact that he grew out of the pure Romantic tradition is invariably clear, and there is great reward in repeated listening. And his finest operas—*Grimes, Screw, Venice,* and *Billy Budd*—always work brilliantly onstage despite the occasional thorniness of the music itself.

Peter Grimes

Prologue, three acts, and Epilogue
First performance: Sadler's Wells Theatre, London, 1945
Libretto: Montagu Slater

In *Peter Grimes,* Britten created one of the most formidable villains in all of opera. No, it isn't the outcast, the somewhat dangerous and occasionally violent and morally ambiguous title character; one gets the feeling that he could, under different circumstances, be rehabilitated. The Great Evil in this work is, rather, the populace of the village in which the opera is set. When the Borough's townsfolk become a mob, they transform from sinister to truly dangerous. Hating Grimes's "differentness," they literally hound him to insanity. When they suspect Grimes of causing his first apprentice's death, his reclusive behavior does nothing to change their opinion. However, one woman, the widow Ellen Orford, espouses Grimes's cause. Together with the kindly Captain Balstrode, she almost changes Grimes's destiny, but he is too much of a pariah and too much a victim of his own tortured mind to be saved. More death will follow.

Britten's obvious identification with Grimes makes the opera work. He and his companion, Peter Pears, were homosexuals and pacifists at a time when both "offenses" were punishable by law. In their own words, they considered themselves "individuals against the crowd." So, in his own way, is the sad, disturbed Peter Grimes.

WHO'S WHO

Peter Grimes, a fisherman (tenor)
Ellen Orford, a schoolmistress (soprano)
Captain Balstrode, a retired skipper (baritone)

WHAT'S HAPPENING

The Borough, a fishing village on the east coast of England, around 1830

The Prologue opens with the inquest into the apprentice's death at sea. Grimes is officially cleared but receives a caution: as a particularly harsh taskmaster, he should employ grown men instead of youths. Ellen Orford raises her voice in support of Grimes against the villagers' outrage.

Act I reveals life in the Borough, underscoring Grimes's isolation from it. When Ellen appears with his new apprentice, a lad from the workhouse, Grimes shows immediately that he is still a hard master.

In Act II, Ellen's own suspicions are aroused when she sees bruises on the boy. She tries to intervene, but Grimes becomes furious. In the second scene of Act II, Grimes accidentally causes the boy's death.

By Act III, the boy's disappearance causes heightened specu-
lation and scorn; even Ellen and Balstrode (previously Grimes's
only supporters) have their doubts. In the Epilogue, the two
come across the now-demented Grimes on the beach, and Balstrode advises him to take himself back out to sea and to sink his
boat. Word comes to the village that a ship has gone down, but
curiosity has dwindled and life goes on as usual.

UNSTIFFENING THE UPPER LIP

In addition to vocal moments, there are four "Sea Interludes"
for orchestra alone. These are orchestral feasts—picturesque, roil-
ing connective tissue within the opera itself, never allowing the
action to flag. These pieces are often played at concerts, out of
context, and they never fail to disturb and fascinate.

Prologue: An off-kilter, brief, very chaste "love duet" for Peter
and Ellen.

Act I: Ellen's lyrical aria "Let her among you without fault
cast the first stone," in which we witness Ellen's strong character
and devotion to Peter in the face of the crowd; Peter's scene "Now
the Great Bear and Pleiades," which he sings as if in a hallucina-
tory trance as he enters the local tavern, making the locals even
more suspicious of him: "He's mad or drunk," they sing.

Act II: Ellen, chorus, and Peter: "This unrelenting work,"
with Ellen accusing Peter of overworking the new apprentice
while the church congregation's offstage service is heard; Peter's
solo in the act's second scene when he's alone in his hut with
the young lad, "Go there! . . . In dreams I've built myself some
kindlier home." The difficult vocal line, composed for Britten's

muse/lover/partner Peter Pears, lies very high and requires perfect enunciation—and is, once again, a type of mad scene, like the scene at the tavern.

Act III: Ellen's aria "Embroidery in childhood was a luxury of idleness," wherein she realizes that Peter is probably guilty of all he has been accused of; and, last, Peter's full-blown mad scene, "Steady. There you are. Nearly home." Here we find Peter pathetically alone onstage for fifteen minutes as he's pursued, offstage, by the townsfolk. He's accompanied only by the occasional foghorn and the chorus, eerily calling his name from a distance.

Italian Opera

IF YOU CAN HUM IT,
IT'S PROBABLY ITALIAN

I've already discussed the origins of Italian opera—which are the origins of opera—in the introduction. Suffice it to say that if you like it instantaneously and can hum a tune having heard it only once, you're listening to Italian opera. In addition, hand-wringing, wildly overt melodrama, rage, forbidden or doomed love, and long-drawn-out deaths are typical of the national profile. In other words, if it strikes you instantly as "operatic" and the passions are as overt as they are in the *Godfather* trilogy or *Goodfellas*, it is probably Italian opera.

Claudio Monteverdi

Claudio Monteverdi (1567–1643) is a composer's composer. In other words, everyday listeners may hardly consider him in the pantheon, but by those who write new music today, he is as much a hero as Beethoven; he was certainly as innovative, connecting sung word with emotion in both church and secular music. Simply put, Monteverdi is the link between the Renaissance style and the Baroque. Though he was once famous mostly for his madrigals, his three extant operas (*L'Orfeo*, *L'Incoronazione di Poppea*, *Il Ritorno d'Ulisse in Patria*) have, in the past thirty-five years, become hot stuff on opera stages, recordings, and DVDs.

L'Orfeo
Prologue and five acts
First performance: Ducal Palace, Mantua, February 1607
Libretto: Alessandro Striggio

L'Orfeo was Monteverdi's first opera and arguably the first opera, period (see page 3). His is a different take on the Orpheus legend from Gluck's (see page 31), in some ways more artificial and "posed" and in others even more moving. The title role requires a low tenor or high baritone who can sing long, long phrases with great beauty—he is charming the powers of Hell, after all. Considering the composer's own legacy—with one foot in the Renaissance and the other in the Baroque—it is fitting that this piece also traces a crucial transition from one world to another.

After you read the synopsis you may be put off; when I see shepherds and nymphs, I run. But what is so glorious about this opera is that the moments of rejoicing are truly joyous, the laments are truly sad; when Orfeo is attempting to sing his way into the Underworld, he sings a wildly virtuosic aria. Even if you have only the barest outline of the plot, you can tell what's going on: in Act II, when the Messenger enters with news of Euridice's death, the music is so picturesque that you know almost before she sings a note that something dreadful has happened. It's really a pity that many of Monteverdi's operas have been lost—he was a great, great dramatist.

By the way, don't be frightened by the fact that the opera is in five acts with a prologue—it comes in at about an hour and forty-five minutes.

WHO'S WHO

La Musica (soprano)
Orfeo (tenor or baritone)
Euridice (soprano)
La Messaggera (Messenger; mezzo-soprano)
Speranza (Hope; soprano)
Caronte (Charon; bass)
Plutone (Pluto; bass)
Proserpina (soprano)
Apollo (tenor)

WHAT'S HAPPENING
Greece, mythological time

Prologue: La Musica (the personification of Music) enters and announces that the story—in music—that we will hear will both stimulate and calm us. She tells us it will be about Orfeo, whose power of singing was mythical.

Act I: Shepherds and nymphs—Orfeo's friends—celebrate the wedding of Orfeo and Euridice. They ask him to sing of his joy and he does, in a hymn to the sun. Euridice expresses her happiness and love, and all go to the temple.

Act II: Orfeo and his friends celebrate their home, the fresh air, and flowers. Suddenly a Messenger appears and announces that Euridice, while out gathering flowers, was bitten by a snake and has died. All lament, and Orfeo vows to go to the Underworld and get Euridice back.

Act III: Led by Speranza, Orfeo gets to the gates of the Underworld (and, as we know from Dante, Hope can go no farther), but Charon, the ferryman, will not row Orfeo across because he is still alive. Orfeo sings to him, and, though unmoved, Charon is so soothed that he falls asleep. Orfeo gets into the boat and crosses the river; a chorus of Underworld spirits ends the act.

Act IV: Orfeo reaches Hades and sees Pluto, the god of the dead, who at first refuses his request but at the bidding of his wife, Proserpina, finally gives in, providing Orfeo leads Euridice out but does not look at her. Orfeo agrees but gives in to doubts about Pluto's promise; he turns and looks into Euridice's eyes. She bids him farewell and returns to Hades as he continues back toward the loving world. A chorus of spirits sings of the soul's virtue.

Act V: Back home, Orfeo bemoans his fate; the hills echo his feelings. He sings again, saying that he will never love another woman again. Apollo, his father, appears and invites him up to the heavens to see Euridice as well as joy and peace. They ascend to the heavens amid singing and dancing.

FAR MORIRE

Prologue: Opening instrumental fanfare on brass and strings, always associated with the Gonzaga family, who were Monteverdi's employers. It may be very brief, but it clearly announces that something grand is about to occur.

Act I: Orfeo's lovely "Rosa del ciel"; the closing chorus, joyful with Orfeo's happiness.

Act II: Orfeo's hymn to the woods "Vi ricorda, o boschi ombrosi" and the sudden, tragically mood-changing entrance of the Messenger; the shepherds' lament, repeated three times, "Ahi, caso acerbo."

Act III: The true heart of the opera is Orfeo's plea to Charon to take him across the river Styx, "Possente spirito e formidabil nume," a long showpiece that becomes more and more florid and challenging to sing as it continues. This is Orfeo strutting his stuff in a most moving, stunning manner.

Act IV: Proserpina's pleas to Pluto to listen to Orfeo—all

done in recitative, but wonderfully like a modern couple having a discussion; the chorus's song of approval; the trip out of Hades.

Act V: Apollo's entrance and Orfeo's ascendancy; the final chorus, "Vanne Orfeo felice a pieno" (Go, Orfeo, happy and ful-filled), and dance.

Gioacchino Rossini

It is appropriate that the life of Gioacchino Rossini (1792–1868) spanned the period between the classical and bel canto operatic styles. After all, he is the man who brought Figaro from Mozart and Da Ponte's sociopolitical satire into the realm of pure oper-atic *buffo brio* in *The Barber of Seville*. As with so many, Rossini's family was mostly musicians (though his father was a butcher as well as a horn player). The young composer experienced an almost prodigy-like success; his first piece, *La Cambiale di Ma-trimonio* (The Marriage Contract), was staged in Venice when he was only eighteen years old. From then on, Rossini enjoyed a string of hits and honors: he was the director of both of Mi-lan's opera houses and all of Naples's, writing *Otello*, *La Ceneren-tola*, *Il Barbiere di Seviglia*, *La Donna del Lago*, *Ermione*, and many other works during this time. In Italy, during his reign as composer (1810–1822) he was the man to beat—and no one did. Next he moved to Paris, where he accepted the most un-Figaro-like titles of Composer to the King and Inspector Gen-eral of Singing. Paris was also where he wrote *Guillaume Tell* (most famous to us today for its overture) and eventually where

A caricature of Gioacchino Rossini, c. 1830, the year after his retirement at age thirty-seven, a big bag of money under his right arm, a piece of paper with the words "Easy music" written on it coming out of his left side pocket, and the Paris Opéra collapsing behind him. What would become of opera after he stopped composing?

he chose to retire at the early age of thirty-seven. The composer spent most of his remaining years entertaining a wide circle of friends, and enjoying France's culinary culture. Tournedos Rossini, a dish made up of filet mignon sautéed in butter and served on a *crouton*, topped with foie gras and truffles, was invented either for him or by him. He also wore two toupees when his apartment was chilly, and he refused to allow a particular tenor into his apartment until the latter had "checked his high C at the door." In all he wrote thirty-eight operas, stealing from himself along the way. Mozart may be the greatest composer who ever lived, but Rossini is the most entertaining.

Il Barbiere di Siviglia (The Barber of Seville)

Two acts
First performance: Teatro Argentina, Rome, 1816
Libretto: Cesare Sterbini

Opening nights of opera are always an event, but that of *Il Barbiere di Siviglia* was a positive comedy of errors. Rossini, conducting from the harpsichord, was wearing a jacket that had been given to him by the management; it was too small for his plump body, and the audience immediately began to laugh. Then a guitar string broke during the tenor's onstage serenade, bringing on more ridicule. When Rosina—a local favorite—made her first, very brief appearance, viewers thought she'd have little to do and became angry. A bit later, Don Basilio tripped and fell, continuing to sing while his nose bled. And when a cat happened onstage and meowed noisily, there was no chance of regaining decorum. But the real reason for the fiasco was probably the fact that Giovanni Paisiello's *Il Barbiere di Siviglia* had been a great favorite, and his fans, angry that Rossini had usurped the plot, came to disrupt the evening. By the second performance, however, all was well. The music was simply too good and the story too delightful to resist. In the subsequent two centuries, *Il Barbiere* has become the most famous and beloved comic opera in the world.

WHO'S WHO

Figaro, a wily barber and factotum (baritone)
Count Almaviva (tenor), known as Lindoro to the woman he loves . . .
Rosina (mezzo-soprano), the ward of . . .
Dr. Bartolo (baritone), who wants her for himself
Don Basilio, a music teacher (bass)

WHAT'S HAPPENING

In Act I, Count Almaviva enlists Figaro's help to win Rosina's affections and to rescue her from Dr. Bartolo, her creepy old guardian (and her even creepier singing teacher, Don Basilio, who is in cahoots with Bartolo). He serenades her, pretending to be a poor student named Lindoro; she is immediately taken with him. When Figaro and the count hear that Bartolo wants to marry her the next day, Figaro suggests that the count infiltrate the house disguised as a drunken soldier looking for lodging. Soldiers arrive when there is a ruckus, and the act ends in confusion.

In Act II, the count reappears at Bartolo's house, disguised as a singing teacher stepping in for the ill Don Basilio. Rosina and the disguised count have fun fooling Bartolo and making plans until Basilio himself shows up. Barely allowed to speak, he is paid off by the count and leaves. Basilio and Bartolo fabricate some evidence that makes Lindoro/the count seem unfaithful, but all is righted when his true identity is revealed and the count and Rosina wed—with great thanks to the cunning barber, Figaro.

FAR MORIRE

Act I: Almaviva's "Ecco, ridente in cielo," an utterly charming, somewhat florid serenade; Figaro's aria "Largo al factotum," possibly the most popular aria in all of opera (you'll recognize it at once) filled with fun jumps and fast singing so picturesque that just hearing the words lets you picture the singer's facial expressions; Rosina's aria "Una voce poco fa," in which she introduces herself as a sweet young thing who always gets what she wants, with lovely roulades and witty vocal explosions; Rosina and Figaro's duet "Dunque io son," in which he realizes just how sharp she is—note how she sings rings around him (almost literally); the ensemble finale, "Fredda ed immobile," during which the singers stand "frozen and motionless," not knowing what will occur next, and then go through a series of noises that they feel are going on in their heads. If you think music cannot be funny, this will prove you wrong.

Act II: Rosina's lesson scene, "Contro un cor," a showpiece aria, really, but in context what Almaviva, dressed as a singing teacher, is presumably helping her with; the ensemble "Don Basilio! . . . Buona sera, mio signore," which takes place when Don Basilio shows up suddenly, uninvited, in the lesson scene and might just ruin the couple's plot; the trio "Ah! Qual colpo . . . Zitti, zitti, piano, piano," in which Almaviva and Rosina declare their love while Figaro urges them to escape. If you're lucky, Almaviva's final aria, "Cessa di più resistere," will be included in whatever performance you see or hear—it's a real attraction, but since it is too difficult for most tenors, it is normally cut.

La Cenerentola (Cinderella)

Two acts
First performance: Teatro Valle, Rome, 1817
Libretto: Jacopo Ferretti

La Cenerentola's opening night was a failure. There was a brutal storm, a baritone who "had the system, when singing, of shouting like a man possessed," and a tenor "whose voice . . . often seemed like a shopful of wrong notes." Even the novelist Stendhal, Rossini's great admirer and first biographer, wrote that most of the music was contaminated by "the odor of money-grubbing, gutter-minded businessmen." Rossini, however, was undaunted. "Fools!" he said to a friend. "It will be fought over by impresarios and even more by *prime donne*." Of course, he was right.

Perhaps the composer's confidence came partially from faith in the power of the classic Cinderella story—though this one is only just recognizable, since almost all the characters are in disguise. Other dissimilarities between opera and familiar tale: there are no vehicular pumpkins, no glass slippers, no stepmother (it's a stepfather who reigns supremely mean). What we do still have are the egalitarian prince, the dreadful stepsisters, and Cinderella, who keeps on turning that other cheek.

Despite its initial failure, by year's end *Cenerentola* was staged in seven other Italian cities, and before Rossini died, it saw productions in English, French, Russian, Polish, Czech, and German, in addition to dozens more in Italian—it was even the first opera ever staged in Australia. Angelina (Cenerentola's real name) is so loving and forgiving (she is treated really badly in the opera; at one point, her father tells an emissary of the prince that she's dead, right in front of her) that we actually love her during the opera. Only Rossini (and Mozart) could turn comedy into quicksilver truth so artfully.

WHO'S WHO

Angelina (aka Cenerentola; mezzo-soprano)
Don Magnifico, Angelina's stepfather (bass)
Clorinda, Don Magnifico's elder daughter (soprano)
Tisbe, Don Magnifico's younger daughter (mezzo-soprano)
Prince Ramiro (tenor)
Dandini, Prince Ramiro's valet (baritone)
Alidoro, Prince Ramiro's tutor (bass)

WHAT'S HAPPENING

Salerno, fairy-tale time

In Act I, Alidoro, the prince's tutor, pays a visit to the seedy castle of Don Magnifico. Since he's disguised as a beggar, the don's froufrou, snobby daughters, Clorinda and Tisbe, do not receive him. But the shabby-yet-sweet Cenerentola does not have such social compunctions, so she welcomes him and gives him something to eat. Courtiers enter to announce the arrival of the prince, who will marry the fairest lady of the house. All except Cenerentola race off to prepare. The prince enters disguised as his own valet, and he and Cenerentola fall for each other; she does not know who he is. Dandini, the prince's valet, enters haughtily, disguised as the prince, and he charms Clorinda and Tisbe while Don Magnifico grovels. Dandini tells Ramiro that the stepsisters are arrogant and charmless. Alidoro returns to outfit Cenerentola for Ramiro's ball, and she makes a grand entrance at the palace, masked and dazzling in her borrowed finery. Everyone is confused as to her identity, and a wild dinner is served.

In Act II, Ramiro, still in disguise, overhears Cenerentola tell Dandini (whom she thinks is the prince) that she is in love with his servant (who is really the prince); overjoyed, he asks for her hand. Instead, she gives him one of the two bracelets she is wearing and tells him to repeat his offer in the light of day. Ramiro, home again, vows to find her. Dandini tells the horrified Don Magnifico who he really is. Back at Don Magnifico's, Cenerentola is back in her rags, and Ramiro, now dressed as himself, arrives and asks shelter from a storm. Ramiro and Cenerentola recognize each other, and the matching bracelets seal their love. Back at the palace, she forgives her family and expresses her joy.

FAR MORIRE

With brilliant creative numbers following quickly one upon the other, almost every minute of this opera is a highlight; these are a few really unbeatable moments.

Act I: Overture, with one of Rossini's great, amusement-park crescendos. Dandini's entrance aria (as the prince), "Come un ape," in which he describes himself as a bee going from flower to flower to choose the best: a great mock-heroic piece. The quintet "Signor, una parola," wherein Cenerentola begs Magnifico to let her go to the ball and he mocks her as the prince and Dandini watch and comment; what begins as a sweet, simple plea becomes a startlingly intricate confrontation, with emotions and lots of little notes flying.

Act II: Ramiro's high-flying aria; the Magnifico-Dandini duet "Un segreto d'importanza," in which Magnifico's rage is matched by Dandini's joy. The sextet, "Siete voi? . . . Questo è un nodo avviluppato," in which the truth is revealed and all sing about being tied in a knot: the music is marked *staccato* and *maestoso* (majestically); each singer starts the same way but begins to riff, while the tune is repeated over and over again by the rest (again, an example that music itself can be funny). Cenerentola's rondo finale, "Nacqui all'affanno," a rightfully famous show-piece; she comments on how fortunes can change in a flash and forgives her family. A rousing closing scene.

Vincenzo Bellini

Vincenzo Bellini (1801–1835) may not have lived long enough
to be elected president of the United States, but he certainly
burned bright in his short time on Earth. "You are a genius,
Bellini," Heinrich Heine remarked maliciously, "but you will
pay for your great gift with a premature death. All the great ge-
niuses die young, like Raphael and like Mozart." And, indeed,
Bellini died of an inflamed intestine (or dysentery) at the age of
thirty-four. Born in Sicily into a musical family, he first studied
in Naples (where his first opera, a student work, and his second
were performed) and then moved to Milan, where he had a
resounding success with *Il Pirata*, his first opera for La Scala.
Norma and *La Sonnambula* were also runaway hits for the young
composer; in all, Bellini left eleven operas (one was a reworking
of an earlier piece). His pure, limpid vocal lines are made up of
melodies which are simply gorgeous; indeed, Richard Wagner,
who, it is said, invented the concept of endless melody, was a
great admirer of Bellini's early in his career, before he began to
loathe everything Italian opera stood for. The publisher Léon
Escudier said that he was "sweet as the angels, young as the
dawn, melancholy as the sunset," though others found him competitive and demanding.

Bellini, along with Donizetti and Rossini, epitomizes the bel
canto style of vocal writing. One would think that all "canto"
should be "bel," but, in fact, there are certain rules for true bel
canto: the singer must have superb breath control, phrase elegantly,

have a flawless legato (the art of seamlessly attaching one note to the next, with no breaks, for an absolutely smooth vocal line), be able to sing very softly throughout the range, have an agile voice capable of fluid coloratura, and so on. And all of this must be at the service of the musical drama. Bel canto ushered in the rise of the soprano as star of the opera stage—and the corresponding decline in roles for castrati singers. Discuss.

Norma

Two acts
First performance: Teatro alla Scala, Milan, 1831
Libretto: Felice Romani

Only tragedy can result when a woman must choose between the man she loves and the people (and gods) she serves. Norma, high priestess of the Druids, long ago took her vestal virgin vows. However, she has also borne two children to Pollione, the Roman who has captured her heart. The character of Norma is, by turns, authoritative, pious, motherly, vengeful, understanding, frightened, warm, rueful, and resigned—and her portrayals have been as varied as the singers who have interpreted the role: Rosa Ponselle had great smoothness of delivery and richness of sound; Gina Cigna added passion; Zinka Milanov's Verdian dignity was impressive; Joan Sutherland's fluency with *fioriture* (embellishments) was magical; Montserrat Caballé's exquisite sound was almost overwhelming.

Now, from our vantage point it is safe to say that one Norma stands above all the others. Maria Callas sang the role more than eighty times between 1948 and 1965. The only singer to project all of the character's many traits, Callas richly fulfilled Bellini's prescription for opera: "Through singing, [it] must make you weep, shudder, die."

WHO'S WHO

Norma, high priestess of the Druid temple (soprano)
Adalgisa, young priestess and Norma's acolyte (soprano)
Pollione, Roman proconsul in Gaul (tenor)
Oroveso, Norma's father (bass)

Norma's dilemma, knife in hand: Should I kill the kids or give them a hug? Can the audience please vote?

WHAT'S HAPPENING

Gaul, first century B.C.

In Act I, Pollione spies on the Druids as they pray for victory over their Roman masters. He is also inflamed with desire for Adalgisa, who has replaced Norma in his affections. Later, in a scene of revelation, Norma learns about her lover's betrayal, Adalgisa learns that this same man is the father of Norma's children, and the women join forces in cursing Pollione.

In Act II, Norma thinks she must kill her children; she cannot, and she asks Adalgisa to care for them. Adalgisa refuses to take them, instead renewing her own vestal vows and attempting to reunite Norma with Pollione. Norma hears that Pollione plans to abduct Adalgisa, and she arranges for him to be burned as a sacrifice to war. However, she makes herself the victim in his place, and Pollione, seeing the nobility of the woman he has rejected, joins her on the pyre.

FAR MORIRE

Act I: Norma's entrance recitative and aria, "Sediziose voci . . . Casta diva": the pinnacle of bel canto, a beautiful, long vocal line, gentle and flowing, with exposed ascents to high notes, followed by a fast section that is florid and dramatic at once—possibly the most beautiful and challenging aria and cabaletta in all of opera. Norma and Adalgisa's duet "O, rimembranza!," in which Adalgisa tells Norma that she is in love and Norma recalls her own early days of love with Pollione with great sadness; the intermingling of voices is miraculous. The trio finale, "Ma di':

l'amato giovane . . . O non tremare . . . Vanne, sì," in which the truth is revealed: Pollione is Adalgisa's lover, and Norma becomes enraged. Theater wedded to music at its most exciting.

Act II: Opening monologue of Norma, as she watches her sleeping children and contemplates murdering them—a portrait of a loving mother's tormented soul; Norma-Adalgisa duet "Mira, o Norma," another ravishing example of blended voices; Norma's vicious revenge scene, the duet "In mia man alfin tu sei," when Pollione is caught and brought before her; the finale, "Qual cor tradisti," which is indescribable in its sheer sadness.

Gaetano Donizetti

Another founding bel canto composer, Gaetano Donizetti (1797–1848) was the most prolific, composing about seventy operas. By the start of the twentieth century he was known for only a handful: *Lucia di Lammermoor*, *L'Elisir d'Amore*, *Don Pasquale*, and *La Favorita*. He composed one of the most celebrated coloratura scenes ever: the heroine's famous, show-stopping mad scene from *Lucia di Lammermoor*. This is ironic, as Donizetti himself eventually lost his mind after a long-running battle with syphilis. Born in Lombardy into impoverished circumstances, the young maestro began composing early. Prolific in the Italian mode, he wrote several operas each year, as well as the usual chamber works and vocal music. Notable works other than *Lucia* include *La Fille du Régiment* (frequently revived as a showcase for singers, including Natalie Dessay), *Anna Bolena*, and *Lucrezia Borgia* (if you notice a theme of strong and/or misunderstood women, you're not wrong). As with so many of his peers, it is interesting to imagine how Donizetti's work might have changed or matured had he lived to a fuller Verdi- or Puccini-esque old age. Would he have grown to love an *Aida*-style spectacle or continued to concentrate on comedies alternating with searing portraits of women pushed over the edge?

L'Elisir d'Amore (The Elixir of Love)

Two acts
First performance: Teatro alla Canobbiana, Milan, 1832
Libretto: Felice Romani

Conditions of opera composition—and performance—were very different in nineteenth-century Italy. When Donizetti accepted the difficult challenge of composing an opera in less than a month for the Teatro alla Canobbiana in Milan (the management had been suddenly let down by another composer), he immediately turned to the fine librettist Felice Romani for help. He wrote, "I give you a week. . . . Bear in mind we have a German *prima donna*, a tenor who stammers, a *buffo* with a voice like a goat, and a French bass who isn't worth much." Consider that today's composers often take years of revision and out-of-town tryouts to complete their magna opera! Luckily, the story was almost a gimme: A sleepy village wakes up when a medicine man sets up shop. He promises a magic cure for unrequited love, and sure enough, the right boy does get the girl. Was the magic nothing more than false courage? Well, yes and no. At any rate, the work has spontaneity and charm galore, and though it has a moment or two—and an aria—of real pathos, it is a delicious comedy of both manners and errors.

Still, when the composer Hector Berlioz attended a performance of *L'Elisir d'Amore* in the third week of its run, he recorded the following in his *Memoirs*: "I found the theater full of people talking in normal voices, their backs to the stage. The singers, undeterred, gesticulated and yelled their lungs out. . . . People were gambling, eating supper in their boxes, etc." And you thought the guy texting behind you at the movies was bad.

WHO'S WHO

Adina, the richest girl in the village (soprano)
Nemorino, her poor admirer (tenor)
Dr. Dulcamara, a quack doctor (bass)
Sergeant Belcore, a swaggering soldier (baritone)

WHAT'S HAPPENING

An Italian village, early nineteenth century

In Act I, Nemorino, mooning over Adina as usual, droops in defeat when the dashing soldier Belcore appears. He rushes to the quack Dr. Dulcamara and spends all his money on an elixir that guarantees love—but it's only wine. When Nemorino gulps it down, his drunken antics drive Adina into a hasty acceptance of Belcore's proposal, driving Nemorino to despair.

Act II, and it's almost wedding time. Nemorino needs more

"elixir," so he signs up with Belcore for the army to get quick cash. In the meantime, his rich uncle has died, leaving him a rich man. The village girls swoon, and Nemorino, thinking their adoration's source is the potion, courts Adina with newfound charm. She spurns Belcore, gets Nemorino out of the army, and gives her heart to the right man at last.

FAR MORIRE

Act I: Just minutes into the opera, Nemorino pines after Adina in "Quanto è bella, quanto è cara," setting the scene for the plot and this character's innocent love; the Nemorino-Adina duet "Chiedi all'aura"; Dulcamara's aria "Udite, udite, o rustici," a patter-song sales pitch to the "country folk" for his elixir: he's a charlatan, but a very entertaining one! The duet between Dulcamara and the gullible Nemorino is funny, poignant, and quicksilvery. And the entire finale of the act, with Nemorino distraught and everyone else laughing and celebrating the Belcore/Adina wedding-to-be, is as rich in musical ideas as it is both dramatically and comedically apt.

Act II: Belcore and Nemorino's duet—Nemorino needs money to buy more of Dulcamara's "elixir" and Belcore offers it to him if he enlists; the opera's most famous aria (and one of the most recognizable arias in all of opera), "Una furtiva lagrima," which always stops the show with its sweet melodic line and utter sincerity.

Lucia di Lammermoor
Three acts
First performance: Teatro San Carlo, Naples, 1835
Libretto: Salvatore Cammarano

Based on Sir Walter Scott's novel *The Bride of Lammermoor*, which, in turn, was based on a true story, this early Romantic opera is most famous for the heroine's oft-referenced mad scene. The "real-life" Lucia lived in seventeenth-century Scotland and was named Janet Dalrymple. She was engaged to Archibald Lord Rutherford, but her family disapproved and her father forced her into a marriage with David Dunbar of Baldoon. On their wedding night, Janet went berserk and stabbed Dunbar. Found the next morning cowering in the fireplace, she said simply, "Take up your bonny bridegroom." She died a few weeks later of undisclosed causes, but Dunbar survived his stabbing (though he perished twelve years later in a fall from his horse—welcome to the 1600s).

In the opera *Lucia di Lammermoor*, the tragic couple's love is doomed from the start. He is a Ravenswood and she is an Ashton—members of warring clans that make the Capulets and the Montagues look peaceful. Ultimately, Lucia goes mad because of her brother Enrico's cruel scheming. Donizetti's librettist, Salvatore Cammarano, stuck close to Scott's novel, though he made Edgardo's end far more operatic—in his family's graveyard, he stabs himself after hearing of Lucia's death. In the novel Scott has him sinking into quicksand, which would have been difficult to stage, although I, for one, would like to see it. At any rate, Lucia's mad scene should—and does—take its rightful and justified place as the opera's most awaited scene, and it can make or break the reputation of a soprano who tries the role.

WHO'S WHO

Lucia (soprano)
Sir Edgardo de Ravenswood, Lucia's lover (tenor)
Lord Enrico Ashton, Lucia's brother (baritone)
Lord Arturo Bucklaw, Lucia's husband (tenor)
Raimondo Bidebent, a chaplain (bass)

WHAT'S HAPPENING

Scotland, 1695

In Act I, Enrico wants to recapture the Ashton family fortune and glory and gain political favor by marrying off his sister, Lucia (who sees ghosts), to the wealthy Arturo. Lucia, however, has promised herself to Edgardo, whose family, the Ravenswoods, are bitter enemies of hers.

In Act II, her secret comes to light when Enrico discovers the letters from her lover and forges one to convince her that Edgardo is unfaithful. Aghast at this revelation and urged on by a trusted chaplain, Raimondo, Lucia, depressed, reluctantly agrees to a forced marriage with Arturo. Edgardo appears just as she is signing the contract and denounces her.

In Act III, after a brief opening scene in which Edgardo and

Enrico trade insults at Edgardo's castle, we return to Lammermoor castle. Lucia emerges from her wedding chamber raving and spattered with blood. She has murdered Arturo and eventually collapses. In the final scene, at the tombs of his ancestors, hearing the bell toll for Lucia's death, Edgardo stabs himself, hoping they can be together at last.

FAR MORIRE

Despite a wonderful opening aria and rousing cabaletta for baritone (Enrico) expressing anger and a thirst for revenge and a grand final double aria for tenor (Edgardo), in which he pines over his own misery and then Lucia's death, just about all of the moments to die for in this opera involve Lucia; if Lucia is not great, there is little reason to perform this opera. So here are some of her high spots.

Act I: Lucia's aria "Regnava nel silenzio . . . Quando, rapito in estasi." In the first part of this double aria, Lucia describes seeing a ghost come out of a fountain: we learn here that she is sort of nuts and impressionable. The mood is faraway and thoughtful, the melody lovely: it is in two verses, the second of which is always embellished by the soprano. "Quando, rapito in estasi" reflects a complete change of mood. Lucia describes (again, twice, with manic embellishments the second time) how Edgardo means everything to her and she can't wait to see him.

Act II: Duet for Lucia and Enrico, in which her depression deepens and her vocal line remains fascinatingly florid. In the sextet "Chi mi frena in tal momento?" Lucia has signed the

Having had a contractual battle with the Met, the soprano Luisa Tetrazzini hoisted herself onto a platform at the corner of Market and Kearny streets in San Francisco on Christmas Eve 1910 and sang to a crowd of two hundred thousand to three hundred thousand people. Pretty crazy, but not as crazy as poor, demented Lucia, knife at her feet.

marriage contract with Arturo at her brother's insistence. At that moment, Edgardo enters, outraged: all express their horror in a remarkable blend of voices and emotions. It is here that Lucia loses her mind.

Act III: Lucia's mad scene, "Il dolce suono." This scene, lasting almost twenty minutes, is one of the major touchstones in all of opera. Mad scenes in opera proliferated in the first half of the nineteenth century, but Lucia's is the model by which all others are judged. Lucia first tranquilly thinks she's speaking to Edgardo and says they will meet by the fountain; then the ghost appears, and she goes wild with fear. She skips to visualizing her wedding and the guests, with candles lit, and sees her future as bright and happy. The previous music has taken bits of melody from the first-act fountain scene as Lucia recalls those moments, but here there is a free cadenza with flute; a lengthy, "improvised" riff without words designed to stagger the listeners and imply lunacy. Lucia then adds a coda, "Spargi d'amaro pianto" (Shed bitter tears), also in two verses. She ends on a brilliant high note (we hope) and then drops dead.

Note: The tenor's solo comes next and closes the opera; if he is mediocre, there is a race for the exits after the mad scene.

Giuseppe Verdi

To many opera fans, Giuseppe Verdi (1813–1901) *is* opera (unless they're Puccini loyalists, though there is a lot of cross-over between the two camps). The composer of *La Traviata*,

Aida, *Il Trovatore*, and a couple of dozen other fine works was both prolific and adored throughout his long life. When thinking about Verdi—as well as other composers whose primary body of work is operatic—it is always important to remember that he is a dramatist as much as a composer. If opera is the ultimate theatrical experience, the best opera composers must master a particularly complex bag of tricks: making sure, of course, that the music is beautiful and varied but also that the story chugs along and is both entertaining and comprehensible; writing show-stopping arias for the main characters (and writing them juicy enough for the best singers to demand the roles) but also making sure that there are enough movement and action onstage so the production doesn't feel like a recital. And all of that comes after finding a librettist, dealing with theater managers and producers, and wrangling with conductors. Verdi, of course, was a master of all of those varied skills. His life spanned almost the entire nineteenth century—his first opera was produced in 1839 and his last in 1893—and by the 1860s there was hardly a civilized country in the world that was not presenting an opera by Verdi.

As he grew older, he was even more adored, especially in Italy. He still is.

Rigoletto
Three acts
First performance: Teatro La Fenice, Venice, 1851

Rigoletto's role as court jester suits his embittered existence. He is a deformed man—a hunchback—and alone except for his daughter, Gilda, whom he is determined to shelter from the cruel caprices of life at court and in particular his employer, the Duke of Mantua. But Rigoletto's fatherly devotion leads indirectly to what he fears the most, and this irony catapults the story to its tragic end.

Details surrounding the creation of *Rigoletto* were, as is not unusual in opera land, complicated. The censors wanted to eliminate the noble Monterone cursing the Duke of Mantua because royalty mustn't be cursed. They also found the entire story immoral and violent. Verdi managed to work his way around every issue while the public avidly followed the intrigue in the newspapers of the day—remember, opera was popular entertainment, and the public was waiting for Verdi's next work. (Look at it as if James Cameron's next movie were given an X rating or banned for political or moral reasons.)

And just days before the supposed premiere, a question was still being asked: was there to be a tenor aria in the last act? No one had heard or seen it—not even the orchestra or the tenor. Verdi was careful to keep it from them, knowing that once his tune was out, it would go viral so quickly that by the time it actually debuted in performance, people would think he had stolen it! And so it was only during the final rehearsals that cast and orchestra heard "La donna è mobile." Of course, Verdi was right. The day after the premiere, everyone in Venice knew the aria and gondoliers were humming it—it became the most popular song of the season. Vital, vivid, and boiling over with memorable tunes, *Rigoletto* never fails to please.

WHO'S WHO

The Duke of Mantua (tenor)
Rigoletto, the duke's jester (baritone)
Gilda, Rigoletto's daughter (soprano)
Count Monterone, a nobleman (baritone)
Sparafucile, an assassin (bass)
Maddalena, Sparafucile's sister (contralto)

WHAT'S HAPPENING

Mantua, sixteenth-century Italy

In Act I, the bitter jester Rigoletto lauds the lechery of the Duke of Mantua and is cursed by Count Monterone, whose daughter has been the duke's most recent victim. (The curse of a father was superstitiously thought to be particularly powerful.) Rigoletto does not know that the duke has also flirted with his own beloved Gilda and won her heart. The scheming courtiers kidnap Gilda, tricking Rigoletto into helping by pretending she is someone else, and then carry her off to the duke.

In Act II, Rigoletto realizes what has happened and swears revenge.

RUFFO AS RIGOLETTO

Titta Ruffo, a great baritone whose real name was Ruffo Titta—could I make this up?—as the court jester Rigoletto. His popularity was on a par with Caruso's; he earned as much money as the great tenor. One of his competitors said of him, "His was not a voice, it was a miracle." Here he is wearing three sets of drapes.

In Act III, seeing that Gilda has fallen in love with her seducer, he arranges for Sparafucile to murder the duke. However, Maddalena convinces her brother to substitute another victim. Gilda, overhearing and determined to save her lover, volunteers. Because she is in disguise, Rigoletto unwittingly orders his daughter's murder. The cursing of a father—*la maledizione*—has been fulfilled.

FAR MORIRE

Act I: The duke's "Questa e quella," a brief, fresh, easygoing tune that perfectly introduces the duke—women, like flowers, are to be plucked and discarded. The duke's music is always charming, but the duke himself is a monster. In Scene ii, Rigoletto's "Pari siamo," in which he compares himself to an assassin with his mocking of others and gives vent to how much he hates his deformity, the courtiers, and everything except Gilda. The duke-Gilda duet (he is disguised as a student) is both sweet and exciting, and "Caro nome," Gilda's reflective aria, is a glorious piece for the innocent girl with spotless staccato high notes and a dreamy manner.

Act II: Rigoletto's aria "Cortigiani, vil razza dannata," in which he denounces the hateful courtiers—one of the most exhausting baritone scenes ever, a heartrending moment that separates the good from the great singing actors; Rigoletto and Gilda's duet "Tutte le feste al tempio" after she has been ravished by the duke.

Act III: The duke's "La donna è mobile" (on almost every tenor's list of favorite arias). The quartet "Bella figlia dell'amore": the duke promises love to Maddalena; Maddalena laughs it off accusing him of mere flattery; outside, listening, Gilda sobs because he used the same words with her; while Rigoletto swears revenge. This is one of the cool things about opera: four people singing at once, with different feelings, creating a perfect, concise scene.

Il Trovatore (The Troubadour)

Four acts
First performance: Teatro Apollo, Rome, 1853
Libretto: Salvatore Cammarano

The plot of *Il Trovatore* has so often been parodied and so often deemed incomprehensible that one forgets how many great stage works are remembered for the effects they have on their audience rather than for the niceties of their plots. Count di Luna and Manrico are on opposite sides in a civil war; they are also rivals for the hand of Leonora. The enemies do not discover they are brothers until too late, an irony that might have changed the course of events. But then there wouldn't have been an opera, would there?

Even with the convoluted storyline, there's hardly an opera lover who isn't affected by *Il Trovatore*. Some are taken by the poetry to be found in its nighttime settings and private, introspective moments, particularly Leonora's arias. Others concern themselves with its perversities: kidnapped, burned babies; the crazed, witchlike character of Azucena. But everyone agrees that the music is unstoppably stunning. "It is easy to perform *Il Tro-*

vatore," said Enrico Caruso. "All you need are the four greatest singers in the world."

WHO'S WHO

Leonora, a lady-in-waiting (soprano)
Azucena, a Gypsy (mezzo-soprano)
Manrico, a troubadour (tenor)
Count di Luna (baritone)
Ferrando, a captain of the guard (bass)

WHAT'S HAPPENING

Spain, fifteenth century

In Act I, Ferrando tells how the count's brother was kidnapped in infancy and murdered by a vengeful Gypsy, who was then burnt at the stake. (This was Azucena's mother—keep this in mind, or you're really in trouble.) Manrico, a mysterious troubadour, enters to rendezvous with Leonora, but no one knows that he is the missing brother. Leonora is in love with him, and the count, who lusts after Leonora, challenges him to a duel.

In Act II, Azucena tells that she was the Gypsy who took Manrico away and raised him as her own. He tries to figure out her ravings but remains confused, as he should be. Meanwhile, Leonora, believing Manrico to be dead, prepares to enter a convent. The count plans to abduct her, but Manrico saves her just in time.

In Act III, Azucena has been captured by the count, and, in trying to free her, Manrico is himself taken prisoner.

The last scene of Il Trovatore: *The evil count, in his best Snidely Whiplash pose, glares at the overdressed Manrico, who has just accused the half-dead Leonora of betraying him as his mother, Azucena, sleeps on a convenient bale of hay. It doesn't seem like much, but it makes quite a racket.*

In Act IV, Leonora pleads with the count to take her and let Manrico go. We see Manrico and Azucena in prison, and when Leonora enters and is accused by Manrico of giving in to the count's dirty advances, she poisons herself. The count executes Manrico, and only then does Azucena reveal her long-kept secret.

FAR MORIRE

Act I: Leonora's aria "Tacea la notte placida . . . Di tale amor." This double aria is another perfect example of word painting with tones. As Leonora describes the quiet night, the words remain placidly, peacefully sung, within a small vocal range; as she explains how she heard the troubadour's voice, her vocal line rises with her excitement; in the aria's second section, which is much faster, she fiercely states that only he can win her heart: to the accompaniment of plucked cellos and trilling violins, the vocal line bounces around with a nervous, almost outraged energy and flies very high.

Act II: Azucena's aria "Stride la vampa" is a description by the crazed Gypsy of a victim being tortured and burnt at the stake—the flickering flames can almost be heard in the opening lines. Count di Luna's aria "Il balen del suo sorriso," an expression of his love for Leonora, with a great deal of tender singing with plush low strings and woodwinds adding to the dreamlike, aristocratic mood: a perfect example of how a frozen moment, a feeling perfectly expressed, can make great sense despite any absurdity of plot going on around it.

Act III: Manrico's aria "Ah sì, ben mio . . . Di quella pira." The first aria is a tender outpouring of love—a throwback to the eloquent, lyrical singing of the bel canto (see "Una furtiva lagrima" from *L'Elisir d'Amore*, page 132); the second, a truly dramatic outburst from Manrico when he hears that Azucena, his mother, is about to be burnt at the stake. The anxiety and resolve are expressed quickly, with choppy, short phrases and flights up to high C for a tenor with real guts. (Verdi didn't write the high C, but it has come to be expected and audiences get very nasty if they don't get it.)

Act IV: The act opens with one of the true gems in the repertoire: if a soprano can sing Leonora's aria "D'amor sull'ali rosee" properly, she can rightfully call herself a "Verdi soprano." The text is common mock-poetic: she asks the sighing wind to transport her love to Manrico and to comfort him but to conceal "the pain in her heart." But it is Verdi's treatment of it that is so astounding and makes an audience hold its breath, with light accompaniment and a vocal line that stretches gently higher and higher. This is followed by the chorus chanting a "Miserere" for the soon-to-be-dead Manrico, over which Manrico sings a farewell and Leonora almost faints from misery, singing descending, mournful phrases. Di Luna arrives, and Leonora begs for Manrico's life ("Mira, di acerbe lagrime"); she promises to give herself to di Luna if she can see Manrico again. The music has the energy of a steam locomotive that moves it forward with great nervousness as Leonora sings flying rings around the count and then surreptitiously drinks poison from a ring, sounding practically giddy. The final scene features a loving, lullaby duet for Azucena and Manrico before (a) Leonora enters and Manrico denounces her, thinking she has betrayed him; (b) Leonora makes her position clear; (c) the count enters and Manrico is dragged away; (d) Leonora drops dead; (e) Manrico is executed offstage; (f) Azucena screams, "You are avenged, O Mother!"; and

(g) the count screams, "Yet I must live!": (a) through (g) takes less than ten minutes. Short, snappy, senseless, and irresistibly exciting.

La Traviata (The Lost One)

Three acts
First performance: Teatro La Fenice, Venice, 1853
Libretto: Francesco Maria Piave

From the London *Times*, August 11, 1856: "An unfortunate young person who has acted the part of a public prostitute . . . coughs her way through three acts and finally expires . . . in a manner which ought to be revolting to the feelings of the spectators."

The outrage was almost universal. Verdi had dared to compose an opera from a work by Alexandre Dumas *fils*, based on the scandalous life of the author's former lover. Alphonsine Plessis had been an exquisite courtesan who died of consumption a mere six years before *La Traviata*'s premiere. Plessis, make no mistake, was not the near-saintly self-sacrificer of novel, play, and opera ("Lying makes my teeth white," she was quoted as saying). The fictional Violetta, by contrast, is a saint in courtesan's clothing, giving up her happiness and even her life to do right (at least according to her own standards) by the man she loves. The Romanticism of the mid–nineteenth century glorified Violetta to poets and composers, even as she remained horrifying to the general public.

The furor died down eventually, and *La Traviata* has become one of the few operas that everyone loves, with its heroine as the ultimate sympathetic character. Note that while Verdi was composing *La Traviata*, he was living with his mistress, whom he later married, but they were shunned by the people in their town. Verdi was no stranger to the scorn of petty, middle-class people, and he loathed it. No wonder he wrote such sympathetic music for his "fallen woman."

WHO'S WHO

Violetta Valéry, a courtesan (soprano)
Alfredo Germont, her lover (tenor)
Giorgio Germont, Alfredo's father (baritone)
Baron Douphol, Alfredo's rival (baritone)

WHAT'S HAPPENING

Paris and the French countryside, 1850

Act I includes the famous Parisian party scene, during which Violetta, currently being kept by Baron Douphol, and Alfredo meet and fall in love, although Violetta tries to pretend that it is merely a passing flirtation.

In Act II, Violetta has renounced her fancy living, and the lovers settle in the countryside together. Alfredo's wealthy family disapproves, so Violetta secretly sells her jewels to support their ménage. Alfredo's father arrives and pleads with Violetta to give up his son for the sake of the family honor; Alfredo's sister is getting married. Even though she knows that she suffers from consumption and that leaving Alfredo will only make her worse, she returns to Paris and takes up with Douphol. Unaware of her true motives, Alfredo appears at a soiree, denounces her, and challenges his rival to a duel.

By Act III, we return to Violetta's chambers, where she lies dying. Germont *père* relents and tells his son of her unselfishness. The lovers reunite, but only briefly, and Violetta dies in Alfredo's arms.

The American soprano Geraldine Farrar as the dying Violetta in La Traviata, *swathed in two acres of pure white silk. She was equally famous as a movie star and has a star on the Hollywood Walk of Fame; a true living legend in her time, she was mobbed by a huge group of women called Gerry-flappers wherever she went. Her many affairs were reported by the press, her husband's bizarre suicide became a scandal, and she wrote an autobiography in which she referred to herself in the third person, praising herself to the skies.*

FAR MORIRE

Act I: The drinking song "Libiamo ne' lieti calici," one of the catchiest and best-known bits of opera. Alfredo and Violetta's duet "Un di, felice, eterea," in which he recalls the moment he fell in love with her in long melodies and she counters, trying to make light of it all, with a much more flippant vocal line—another example of music's ability to say what words can only suggest. Violetta's double aria "Ah! Fors' è lui . . . Sempre libera," a tour de force of, first, lovely, introspective legato singing and then coloratura fireworks—again showing the two sides of Violetta's personality: truly loving and trying to avoid love and commitment; acting through music at its most artful.

Act II: After Alfredo sings a nice aria about how happy he is, he leaves, and his father enters. The Violetta-Germont duet "Dite alla giovine." This is a heartbreaking piece. It is said that Verdi's most beautiful music is not for lovers but for fathers and daughters; he lost a daughter when she was an infant. The warmth these two characters feel for each other is palpable, with melodies intertwining and harmonies close and loving.

Act III: Violetta's aria "Addio del passato"; the Violetta-Alfredo duet "Parigi, o cara"; the tear-filled finale in which all the characters regret the catastrophe that has befallen them.

Un Ballo in Maschera (A Masked Ball)

Three acts
First performance: Teatro Apollo, Rome, 1859
Libretto: Antonio Somma

This is one of Verdi's most lyrical middle-late masterpieces. There's almost not a note or moment wasted, the story is well told and moves along at a fine clip, and there's actually suspense. It's also brimming with good tunes in arias, duets, and many ensembles. And despite the royal—or gubernatorial—setting, the themes of political intrigue, loyalty, fidelity, and friendship are universal, making the characters' plights ring true.

The story is based on a real incident that occurred in Sweden in 1792: the assassination of King Gustav III. It was originally set in Stockholm, with the Swedish names as given below, but Verdi ran into trouble with the censors. Regicide was never to be portrayed onstage, particularly in nineteenth-century Italy. (The Roman censors also disliked dancing onstage.) Verdi was forced to try alternatives. He at first wanted *Ballo* presented in the kingdom of Naples, so he reset the opera in Pomerania, with a fictitious duke at its center. But after he arrived in Naples to begin rehearsals on the very day of an assassination attempt against Napoleon, the censors demanded such complete alterations that Verdi withdrew the opera rather than submit. The more liberal Rome accepted it set in Boston—a very faraway place to the Italians— and what was a governor, anyway? When *Ballo* was presented in Paris in 1861, it was set in Florence; and in London, it was set in Naples. Nowadays, it is set in either Boston or Sweden—wherever set designers and impresarios want to put it—and nobody much cares who gets killed where. The whole point is moot: the historic Swedish Gustav III was as gay as a Halloween party and would certainly not have been cuckolding his male best friend.

Of course, sticking to the facts wouldn't allow us to have much of an opera, or perhaps it would have been funnier.

WHO'S WHO

Riccardo, Governor of Boston (tenor) [Gustav III], in love with . . .

Amelia (soprano), wife of . . .

Renato, his friend and counsel (baritone) [Jacob Johan Anckarström]

Ulrica, a fortune-teller (contralto) [Madame Arfvidsson]

Oscar, Riccardo's page (soprano)

WHAT'S HAPPENING

Boston or Sweden, late eighteenth century.

In Act l, Riccardo (Gustav III) is so engrossed in his desire for Amelia that he pays little heed to Renato's (Anckarström's) warnings of political intrigue. It is also Renato who steps forward in Scene ii when the fortune-teller Ulrica (Arfvidsson) predicts that the next man to take Riccardo's hand will be his murderer. Aware that Renato is both loyal and oblivious to the romance between Amelia and himself, Riccardo makes light of the warning.

In Act II, Amelia tries to exorcise her love for Riccardo with Ulrica's "cure" of herbs she must gather at midnight under a scaffold. Riccardo meets her there, but they are interrupted by Renato, who has come to offer protection. He does not recognize the heavily veiled woman as his wife until conspirators leap out and tear off her disguise.

Act III reveals a bitter and vengeful Renato. He joins the conspirators and, at a masked ball, forces Oscar, Riccardo's page, to point out the mask that conceals his master's face. Renato kills Riccardo, fulfilling Ulrica's prophecy.

FAR MORIRE

Act I: Renato's aria "Alla vita che t'arride": filled with long melodies and the nicely jaunty, everybody-sings finale of the first scene; in Scene ii, Ulrica's spooky incantation "Re dell'abisso, affrettati," with its low, baritonal notes for mezzo-soprano; Riccardo's catchy aria "Di' tu se fedele," which he sings in the guise of a sailor.

Act II: Amelia's aria "Ecco l'orrido campo," in which she prays for guidance, and Riccardo and Amelia's duet "Teco io sto": both showpieces, filled with the passion that makes Italian opera tick. In the duet, he sings a verse first, she follows, and then they sing together, climbing higher and higher and ending on a blazing high C for tenor and soprano.

Act III: Amelia's aria "Morrò, ma prima in grazia," in which she pleads to see her child, with an audible sob in the vocal line; Renato's angry aria "Eri tu," in which he expresses his hatred for Riccardo ("It was you who soiled the soul of my wife, my love"); in Scene ii, Riccardo's aria "Forse la soglia attinse," in which he vows never to see Amelia again and to appoint Renato to a post far away, with Amelia. And, of course, the scene at the masked ball and the murder, which actually work dramatically.

Don Carlo

Five (later four) acts
First five-act performance: Opéra de Paris, Paris, 1867
First four-act performance: Teatro alla Scala, Milan, 1884
Libretto: Joseph Méry and Camille du Locle

Don Carlo is Verdi's least conventional hero, both musically and emotionally. Because he has only a single brief solo, we get to know him through his duets: with Rodrigo, Elisabetta, Eboli, and so forth. On the emotional side, personal jealousies and political intrigue thrust Don Carlo into escalating conflicts. He falls in love with a French noblewoman, Elisabetta, only to learn that she is destined to become the bride of his father. At the height of the Reformation, he chooses to side with Protestant apostates, coming into still more conflict with his father *and* the Church. Throughout, we like Don Carlo, feeling his plight. He wants to love Elisabetta but isn't permitted to; he wants to be a political hero, but he hasn't the strength or wherewithal. While the historic Don Carlo was a slightly deformed, slightly retarded and cruel misfit, Verdi and his librettists turned him into a hero in their opera. And, like the best heroes, he remains unfulfilled to the end of the piece.

Many feel that this is Verdi's most sophisticated opera, with themes grander and more philosophical than are found anywhere else in the repertoire, and certainly with characters who are three-dimensional.

WHO'S WHO

Elisabetta de Valois, later to be Queen of Spain (soprano)
Princess Eboli, her lady-in-waiting (mezzo-soprano)
Filippo II, King of Spain (bass)
The Infante Don Carlo, his son and heir to the Spanish throne (tenor)
Rodrigo, his friend (baritone)
The Grand Inquisitor (bass)

WHAT'S HAPPENING

France and Spain, 1650

In Act I, Don Carlo goes to France to claim Elisabetta, promised to him as part of a peace treaty. They are delighted to discover that this arranged marriage will also be a union of love. However, their ecstasy is short-lived as King Filippo declares that he will take his son's place at the altar.

Back in Spain in Act II, Rodrigo tries to help Don Carlo with both his political and romantic endeavors. However, he bungles a message and misleads Princess Eboli into thinking it is she Carlo loves. Rodrigo also confers with the king, believing he can influence his thinking and further Don Carlo's causes; the king warns him not to rebel any further.

Act III brings a secret meeting between Carlo and the woman he thinks is Elisabetta but is actually Eboli, who realizes that Carlo loves his stepmother and threatens to betray them to the king. In the meantime, Flemish Protestants are about to be burned at the stake. When Carlo sides with them, the king declares him a traitor. Rodrigo, to all appearances a turncoat, disarms Carlo and wins Filippo's favor.

During Act IV, the lonely King Filippo attempts to face down the Church's Grand Inquisitor, who wants Carlo punished, and he realizes that the throne must always bow to the Church. He also uncovers the love affair between his wife, Elisabetta, and his imprisoned son, while Elisabetta realizes that Filippo has been carrying on with Princess Eboli. The scene changes to Carlo's dungeon, where Rodrigo shows up, prepared to take the blame for the Flemish fiasco so that Carlo can be released and pardoned. Before that can happen, Rodrigo is shot and the king arrives to offer his son freedom on royal terms.

Carlo refuses and, in Act V, escapes to the monastery where his grandfather, Emperor Charles V, is entombed. Elisabetta is there as well, and she and Carlo share what they think is a last embrace. When the king and the Grand Inquisitor arrive to make their arrest, Charles V (or a monk in disguise) materializes and leads Carlo into the cloister's safe haven.

FAR MORIRE

The opera was originally written in and performed in French; it was later translated into Italian, and the first act was eliminated; Verdi later added and cut. The synopsis and highlights that I describe here are for a five-act version, but with the revised Italian text, which remains more familiar than the French.

Act I: Carlo's brief aria, in which he exclaims that he saw his bride-to-be and fell in love with her; Carlo and Elisabetta's duet, "Di qual amor," which is both elegant and subtle.

Act II: The Carlo-Rodrigo duet "Dio, che nell'alma infondere" in which they swear eternal friendship to a majestic tune that occurs frequently during the opera; in Scene ii, Eboli sings a Moorish love song, the exotic "Veil Song." Carlo and Elisabetta, left alone, sing "Io vengo a domandar grazia," a stunning duet that is complicated by the fact they clearly love each other but Elisabetta cannot acknowledge it, since she is married to his father; Carlo faints halfway through it, and she comforts him before he rushes away in horror at the situation's hopelessness.

Act III: The auto-da-fé scene—the burning of heretics: a pageant interrupted by Carlo's challenge to his father, King Filippo, which turns into a complex emotional and musical ensemble as Carlo is taken prisoner.

Act IV: This is one of the most perfect acts in all of Verdi: Filippo's aria "Ella giammai m'amo" shows us the vulnerable monarch, anxious over his position and the fact that his wife never loved him—a humanizing moment for a difficult character. The following scene between Filippo and the Grand Inquisitor is a monstrous battle of wills, with two bass voices (and a bass clarinet in the orchestra) rising tone by tone in anger as the Inquisitor demands the life of Rodrigo, whom he sees as a traitor to the Church. Eboli's aria "O don fatale" is a mezzo-soprano showpiece, with a huge, two-octave range that always stops the show. And last, Rodrigo's death scene—he is shot while visiting Carlo in prison—which has one of the saddest and most dignified melodies.

Act V: Elisabetta's aria "Tu che le vanità," a ten-minute scene in five parts: an invocation to the spirit of Charles V to weep for her; an introspective moment while she awaits Carlo and feels that she will soon die; a lighter memory of her days in France, especially when she first met Carlo; a farewell to youth and false hope, a prayer for death, and, again, an invocation to Charles V. Every aspect of her personality is in this scene—a remarkable psychological portrait.

Aïda

Four acts
First performance: Khedival Opera House, Cairo, 1871
Libretto: Camille du Locle, translated into Italian by Antonio Ghislanzoni and the composer

When the Khedive of Egypt invited Verdi to compose a grand opera for Cairo's Khedival Opera House, the composer declined. However, he competitively caved when he saw a letter suggesting that if he, Verdi, were not interested, then "Wagner might do something really good." After delays, *Aïda* was unveiled, and the production was more than lavish: Radames' shield and helmet were cast of solid silver, and more than three hundred people were onstage. The audience was packed with European and Egyptian glitterati, with the Khedive's harem alone filling three loges. Verdi stayed away, writing that the occasion made him feel "disgust and humiliation" and that his opera had become "no longer art . . . [but] a pleasure party, a hunt." However, he was being cranky as usual. The success of the opera made him even richer and more famous than he already was—which is saying a great deal.

Aida is one of the operas that everyone knows (it is occasionally performed with elephants during the huge second-act pageant), and it is unarguably great in many ways. But it is probably nobody's favorite. It is considered the quintessentially grand opera because of the huge triumphal scene, but, in fact, most of its best music is in introspective arias and one-on-one confrontations, each of which is a gem. Oddly, people are rarely moved (as in "to tears") by *Aida* as they are by many other operas (*La Bohème*, *La Traviata*); they're bowled over, they feel as if they've had a great night at the theater, they have strong opinions about what they've seen, but it's rare that this opera touches the heart. Maybe that's just a personal viewpoint, but I doubt it: the characters are interesting but not the types we hang out with.

WHO'S WHO

Aida, an Ethiopian princess (soprano), enslaved by . . .

Amneris, an Egyptian princess (mezzo-soprano), who is in love with . . .

Radames, the Egyptian captain of the guard (tenor), who loves Aida and not Amneris

Amonasro, the King of Ethiopia in disguise, Aida's father (baritone)

WHAT'S HAPPENING

Egypt at the time of the pharaohs

Act I opens with news that the Ethiopian army is approaching the Valley of the Nile. Radames is ceremoniously given command of the Egyptian troops, and Aida wishes she could cheer simultaneously for her lover and her homeland.

Amneris ushers in Act II with preparations for honors due the triumphant Radames. She wants him for her own, even after she discovers he has the hots for her slave girl and vice versa. As Radames returns in triumph and everyone makes a big deal out of it, he longs to ask for Aida's hand in marriage; instead, the king offers Amneris.

Act III opens on a secluded bank of the Nile, where Aida waits to fret and whine with Radames. Her father, Amonasro, appears and bullies her into believing that the only way she can be united with her lover, her home, and her family is to trick Radames into betraying his army. She succeeds, and Amneris overhears everything. Radames is arrested as Aida and her father flee.

In Act IV, Amneris overcomes her jealousy and offers to rescue Radames. He refuses, choosing to be buried alive over life without Aida. When we last see him, he is entombed—and who do you suppose sneaked in? Aida, with him now, and for all eternity.

FAR MORIRE

Act I: "Celeste Aida," Radames's opening aria, which is feared by most tenors like the plague, as it must be sung two minutes after they enter; Aida's "Ritorna vincitor," where she tries to reconcile her feelings for her lover and her country—big vocal range, big drama.

Act II: The triumphal scene, filled with great noise and excitement—with or without elephants.

Act III: Aida's "O patria mia": in addition to being a heart-rendingly lovely piece, it terrifies sopranos with its (hoped-for) ascent to an extremely tricky quiet high C. Sopranos who otherwise shone in the role gave it up because of that one note: if sung properly, it is like a rainbow. And a double duet for our heroine—first with her father, in which she capitulates, then with her lover, whom she betrays.

Act IV: Amneris's judgment scene, in which she realizes with horror that her spite is about to kill her boyfriend. This is the princess's final and most gleaming moment, requiring a mezzo-soprano of great power at both ends of her range and with real dramatic conviction (her desperation gives us the chance to actually identify with a character in this piece); "O terra addio," a lovely, soft, in-tomb final death duet for our couple.

Otello

Four acts
First performance: Teatro alla Scala, Milan, 1887
Libretto: Arrigo Boito

Verdi's *Otello* is a distillation of Shakespeare's tragedy about the devastations of jealousy. Iago's jealousy translates into evil cunning; Otello's plays itself out in a murderous fury. Although both men are responsible for Desdemona's death, Otello has acted out of misplaced trust and a surfeit of passion (he "loved not wisely but too well," as Shakespeare said), while Iago's actions are malignity in search of a motive. The title role is the ne plus ultra of Italian dramatic tenor roles; only a handful of singers have succeeded in it in the last fifty years, and they are always roundly lauded. If you compare that with the plethora of tenors who are ready and able to sing Nemorino, the Duke of Mantua, or any number of other great tenor parts, the accolades come into perspective.

The contribution of the librettist Arrigo Boito to *Otello*'s success is arguably almost as great as Verdi's. Boito's version is about one-quarter the length of Shakespeare's, but somehow he loses nothing. Eliminating the Bard's entire first act, the action begins and ends in Cyprus; Desdemona's father, the duke, and Brabantio are also excised. The piece now begins in the middle of a storm, creating what is assuredly one of the most stunning opening tableaux in all of opera. What was needed from Act I—some Rodrigo/Iago dialogue to clarify motivation, Otello's and Desdemona's remembrances of their courtship—is very effectively woven in, with the latter becoming part of Verdi's most beautiful love duet. And when Boito wrote original passages, such as Otello's twelve-bar entrance, which establishes him as a great hero (as well as a great tenor), and Iago's evil-personified "Credo," the invention is brilliant. The Boito-Verdi collaboration remains, along with those of da Ponte–Mozart and Hofmannsthal–Strauss, one of the most satisfying in operatic history. *Otello* is a nerve-shattering experience live, and once you've experienced it, it works almost as well on recordings.

WHO'S WHO

Otello the Moor, Governor of Cyprus and general in the Venetian army (tenor)

Desdemona, his wife (soprano)

Iago, Otello's ensign (baritone)

Emilia, Iago's wife and Desdemona's lady-in-waiting (mezzo-soprano)

Cassio, Otello's lieutenant (tenor)

Roderigo, young nobleman (tenor)

WHAT'S HAPPENING
Cyprus, late fifteenth century

In Act I, a crowd waits for the return of the victorious general—along with the scheming Iago and Roderigo. Iago despises Otello for promoting Cassio to a higher rank, and Roderigo wants Otello's wife for himself. Later, Iago contrives a fight between Roderigo and Cassio, causing Otello to rescind Cassio's post.

In Act II, Iago, however, is not satisfied, and he thickens his evil plot. Convincing Cassio to engage Desdemona's aid in restoring his command, he brings Otello to the scene and succeeds in arousing in him the most evil suspicions.

At the start of Act III, Iago plants Desdemona's handkerchief on Cassio. Otello recognizes it as belonging to his wife, and, in Act IV, he murders her. Then, too late, Emilia and Cassio produce evidence of Desdemona's innocence. As Iago flees the scene, Otello needs to hear no more. He stabs himself.

FAR MORIRE

The usual question arises: What's better, the movie or the book? Or, in this case, the opera or the play? Many people think that Verdi's opera is actually better than Shakespeare's play, and I agree: it is trimmed down; action can be telescoped because of that peculiarly operatic convention, the ensemble, where a half-dozen feelings come out at once; and Verdi's music underpins each change in mood, each sensation. When Iago taunts Otello in Act II by mimicking his words, he does so by also mimicking his musical notes: the effect is true mockery. As the opera goes on, I cannot think of a more powerful representation of a man's dignity and honor disintegrating in front of our eyes.

Act I: Otello's opening cry, "Esultate!," showing the warrior—and the tenor—in all his glory in less than thirty seconds; Iago's "Inaffia l'ugola!," a showy, seemingly good-natured drinking song designed to get Cassio drunk, with nasty asides from Iago that show us how manipulative he is; the Otello-Desdemona duet "Già nella notte densa," ten minutes of sheer bliss—the only truly happy moments they share in the whole opera.

Act II: Iago's "Credo," an oath to do evil; Otello's aria "Ora e per sempre addio," a farewell to peace, happiness, and contentment, as he believes Desdemona is unfaithful; the Otello-Iago duet "Si, pel ciel," a vengeance duet that is terrifying in its resolve and viciousness.

Act III: The duet of Otello and Desdemona "Dio ti giocondi," in which Otello's rage mounts and mounts until he calls Desdemona a whore and pushes her out, horrified. The ensemble finale, "A terra! sì . . . nel livido fango": the culmination of jealousy and rage: Otello humiliates Desdemona and throws her to the ground in front of the entire court and the Venetian ambassador; all plead for mercy until Otello collapses, having a seizure.

Act IV: Desdemona's "Willow Song" and "Ave Maria," essentially her farewell to the world, sad, resigned, hopeless; Otello's final scene, "Niun mi tema," after he realizes he has been duped and has wrongly killed Desdemona. He kills himself as the music of the first-act love duet is played by the orchestra.

Amilcare Ponchielli

Amilcare Ponchielli (1834–1886) had the poor luck to come right after his country's four greatest composers: Rossini, Bellini, Donizetti, and, most specifically, the omnipresent Verdi. He entered the Milan Conservatory with great promise at the age of nine, but his early career hardly lived up to such potential. In 1856 he composed his first opera, *I Promessi Sposi*, but it was a flop. He took jobs in small towns, and in Piacenza and Cremona was named bandmaster, a job consisting of arranging and composing works for wind band. He eventually composed more than two hundred of these—funeral marches, celebratory political pieces, and a concerto for euphonium, a sort of minituba whose sole purpose would appear to be to be the butt of jokes: Q: What do you call a euphonium player with a pager and a cell phone? A: Optimistic. And Q: What's the difference between a dead euphonium player and a dead snake? A: The snake died on its way to a gig. But in 1872 he revised *I Promessi Sposi* and the powerful music publisher G. Ricordi offered him a contract that also brought attention from La Scala. In 1876 La Scala presented *La Gioconda* to great acclaim, although the version we hear today was revised several times and finally appeared in 1880. In 1881 he was named professor at the Milan Conservatory; two of his pupils were Puccini and Pietro Mascagni. He wrote several other operas, a couple of which were successful, and he was well respected as an orchestrator, but now he is remembered almost solely for the blood-and-thunder *La Gioconda*.

La Gioconda (The Smiling One)

Four acts
First performance: Teatro alla Scala, Milan, 1876
Libretto: Arrigo Boito (writing as "Tobia Gorrio")

Opera doesn't get much grander, more hot-blooded, or less subtle than *La Gioconda*. The first act takes place in the courtyard of the Doge's Palace in Venice; the second act, set at sea, offers a ship in flames; the third act is set in the Ca' d'Oro (the "House of Gold," one of the most sumptuous fifteenth-century palaces in Venice); and the final act calls for no less than a ruined palace on an island. In addition, six top-notch singers are required—one in each major voice category—and, of course, there's the third-act ballet ("Dance of the Hours," famously animated in Disney's *Fantasia*). *Gioconda's* music is tuneful and accessible, and the action runs almost nonstop. Gioconda, the eponymous heroine, is very busy, with actions that keep both the plot and the other characters trotting along. The great joke, of course, is that her name means "the smiling one" (like the *Mona Lisa*), and all she has is trouble and sacrifice. She adores her blind, pious mother, whom the villain, Barnaba, tries to have burned as a witch; she loves Enzo, but he "just wants to be friends," preferring the hot Laura, who is married to Alvise; and at the end of the opera, she takes poison rather than submitting to the hellish, sex-filled advances of Barnaba.

So what more could anyone want? Well, here's a hint: the great American dramatic soprano Lillian Nordica, after she had sung the title role nearly seventy-five times, confessed that she had no idea what the opera was about! The librettist, Arrigo Boito, better known for writing the libretti for Verdi's *Otello* and *Falstaff*, used a pen name for *La Gioconda*. A wise career move, perhaps? The opera's final line is a pip. Just as Barnaba is about to ravish Gioconda, she stabs herself, but before he realizes that she is, in fact, dead, he yells, "Yesterday your mother offended me, so I strangled her." Then, realizing he is screaming at a corpse, he finishes with "She doesn't hear me! Aaargh!"

To die for, indeed.

WHO'S WHO

Gioconda, a street singer (soprano)
Enzo Grimaldo, the Genovese nobleman she loves (tenor)
La Cieca, Gioconda's blind mother (contralto)
Alvise Badoero, a leader of the state Inquisition (bass)
Laura Adorno, Alvise's wife, in love with Enzo (mezzo-soprano)
Barnaba, a spy of the Inquisition and an admirer of Gioconda (baritone)

WHAT'S HAPPENING

Venice, seventeenth century

Act I opens on a festive street scene. Barnaba woos Gioconda, and when she spurns him, he denounces her mother as a witch. Gioconda pleads with Alvise for mercy; Laura (wearing a mask) kindly intercedes, and Gioconda's mother is spared. During the excitement, Gioconda's beloved Enzo appears, in disguise to foil his enemies. He recognizes Laura, his youthful love, who was forced to marry his archenemy, Alvise.

In Act II, Barnaba arranges a shipboard rendezvous between Laura and Enzo, hoping to get rid of Enzo for good by revealing all to Alvise. Gioconda learns of the meeting and sneaks aboard, prepared to kill for love. However, when she sees that Laura is the woman who saved her mother, she helps her rival escape.

By Act III, Alvise has learned of Laura's unfaithfulness and commands her to take poison. However, Gioconda substitutes a sleeping draft.

In Act IV, to free the imprisoned Enzo, Gioconda promises herself to Barnaba in exchange. She contemplates another attempt to do away with Laura but changes her mind, arranging safe passage for the lovers. She then kills herself before Barnaba can claim her.

FAR MORIRE

In the first act, as Gioconda is leaving the scene after the ensemble in which her mother has been pardoned, she sings "Madre! Enzo adorato! O, come t'amo!" On the words "t'amo" (I love you), Ponchielli asks the soprano to rise to an almost whispered high B flat—a treacherous, exposed note—to stunning effect; the great soprano Rosa Ponselle used to say that if that note worked right, the rest of the evening would be just fine.

Act I: "Enzo Grimaldi, Principe di Santafiore" is a duet for Barnaba and Enzo; the former recognizes the latter even though he is in disguise and he promises to get Laura to his ship. It's a thrilling tenor-baritone moment: tense, mellifluous, soaring—and filled with Enzo's love and Barnaba's nastiness.

Act II: Barnaba's barcarolle, a fisherman's ballad (he's in disguise); Enzo's evocative aria "Cielo e mar," one of the touchstones of the tenor repertoire; his love duet with Laura; the Laura-Gioconda duet "È un anatema!," in which they both declare their love for Enzo ("I love him as the lion loves blood," sings the gentle Gioconda). Written for two huge voices, it has been described as "two elephants sliding down a banister." It certainly is thrilling.

Act III: The Alvise-Laura duet, a noisy piece in which she pleads for her life and he makes her take poison; the ensemble/finale "Già ti veggo, immota e smorta," sung when the gathered guests are shown Laura's (presumedly) dead body. Enzo tries to kill Alvise and is arrested; Gioconda agrees to give herself to Barnaba in exchange for Enzo's life; Barnaba grabs Gioconda's blind mother, who has somehow wound up in the same place, and drags her out of the room.

Act IV: The entire fourth act is a melodramatic mishmash perfectly worthy of what has come before it and contains great, great over-the-top, near-hysterical music. Gioconda contemplates "Suicidio" in a long aria, her voice rising when she thinks of the happy hours that floated by with her mother, whom she has momentarily misplaced (remember, Barnaba stole her at the end of the third act?) and booming when she thinks of the grave, which she longs for. Enzo arrives and calls her "a raging hyena" at one point, but mind-bogglingly, when he realizes that Gioconda has saved Laura, who starts to sing just as he is about to stab Gioconda, the three sing a marvelous trio and the lovers leave. But there's more: Barnaba arrives to have his way with Gioconda, and she manages to sing girlish coloratura around him before she drops dead. Priceless.

Pietro Mascagni

The great work of Pietro Mascagni (1863–1945) is *Cavalleria Rusticana*. Usually its one act is staged on a grand scale, with scores of chorus members, live animals, and sumptuous sets, and is paired with Leoncavallo's *Pagliacci* (though the combo's nickname, "Cav and Pag," sounds more like a comedy team than the two seminal works of operatic *verismo*). Born in Tuscany to a father who was a pizzeria owner, the composer was full of contradictions: he was a devoted husband and father who also kept a long-term mistress (Anna Lolli, a strikingly beautiful singer) and children holed up in Rome; as temperamental and despairing as any of his characters, he also enjoyed great love and devotion from the Italian public. Mascagni and Giacomo Puccini were roommates as conservatory students and enjoyed a lifelong—if sometimes contentious—friendship.

Cavalleria Rusticana (Rustic Chivalry)

One act
First performance: Teatro Costanzi, Rome, 1890
Libretto: Giovanni Targioni-Tazzetti and Guido Menasci

Most people consider *Cavalleria Rusticana*, with its ruthless realism, the epitome of brutality on the opera stage. Just consider the story: It is Easter in a rustic village, but the passions that erupt are far from holy. When the soldier Turiddu returns from war to find his beloved Lola now wed to another man, nothing can make him give her up—neither her married state nor his own involvement with a local girl, Santuzza, who is pregnant with his child. As the opera draws to a close, Turiddu sings a farewell to his mother and then goes offstage, where Lola's husband, Alfio, out of view, kills him.

As awful as this is, *Cavalleria* could have been worse, considering what happens at the end of the story upon which the opera is based: Alfio challenges Turiddu to a duel, and then he throws dust in his face, momentarily blinding him. While blinded, Alfio stabs Turiddu in the throat and stomach, and he laughs at Turiddu's mother, who will have no son to help her. The blood burbles out of Turiddu's throat so violently that he "could not even gasp." Where is Martin Scorsese when we need him?

WHO'S WHO

Turiddu, a young soldier (tenor)
Santuzza, a village girl (soprano)

Alfio, a village carter (baritone)
Lola, Alfio's wife (mezzo-soprano)
Mamma Lucia, Turiddu's mother (contralto)

WHAT'S HAPPENING
A village in Sicily, late nineteenth century

Turiddu serenades Lola outside her own house before dawn. A bit later, Alfio, unaware of their tryst, looks for Turiddu elsewhere. Santuzza covers for Turiddu and warns Mamma Lucia to do the same. After the townspeople have gone to church, Santuzza begs Turiddu to be kind and return to her, but he casts her aside. Spurned, she tells Alfio about his wife's betrayal, though she instantly regrets her indiscretion, knowing that a duel will necessarily follow. Alfio and Turiddu fight, and the ending shadows the beginning, with Santuzza and Mamma Lucia joined in their concern for Turiddu. But this time, he is beyond their aid. As the women embrace, a voice calls out to announce his death.

FAR MORIRE
Turiddu's serenade "O Lola," sung offstage before anyone enters, a simply lovely little love song; Easter chorus with Santuzza's solo "Inneggiamo," a soul-stirring piece of religiosity, particularly in the context of her excommunication; Santuzza's aria "Voi lo sapete," in which she tells Turiddu's mother about their affair and his relationship with Lola; the Santuzza-Turiddu duet "Tu qui, Santuzza?," in which he repeatedly tells her that he cannot stand her and she just keeps groveling—until she tells him to beware

and curses him; Turiddu's "Mamma, quel vino e generoso," a wildly sentimental, melodramatic farewell to his mother—and a tenor's pride and joy.

Ruggero Leoncavallo

Imagine: all of our feelings about Mimì and Rodolfo and their doomed love might be wrapped up in the music of Ruggero Leoncavallo (1857–1919) if Puccini hadn't written *La Bohème* first. *Pagliacci*, Leoncavallo's big hit, has spawned a small cottage industry of inspired tributes, from Federico Fellini's entire oeuvre (think of *La Strada*'s tragic circus folk or any of the characters in *The Clowns*) to Smokey Robinson's Motown masterpiece "Tears of a Clown" ("Just like Pagliacci did, I try to keep my surface hid"). The Neapolitan composer didn't realize that his short, taut opera would be such a longtime favorite; his ambitions and accomplishments were far larger than *Pagliacci*'s small scale. He wrote many operas and operettas over the course of his life, but it is for the tragic clown that we remember him. See it as the epitome of melodrama whose searing, heart-wrenching music is not easily forgotten. Along with *Cavalleria Rusticana*, with which it is almost always paired (each is less than seventy-five minutes long), it's an audience favorite—a fine evening of high drama and bloodshed.

Pagliacci (Clowns)

Two acts (performed as one)
First performance: Teatro dal Verme, Milan, 1892
Libretto: Written by the composer

While most famous for the sad clown's self-pitying, tragic aria "Vesti la giubba" (picture a clown putting on whiteface makeup and crying, and you've got it), *Pagliacci*'s set piece is actually the commedia dell'arte play-within-a-play, which takes up the last fifteen minutes of the opera, epitomizing the piece's themes: the merging of fantasy and reality due to insane anger and jealousy, the transformation of simple farce into high tragedy. Stylistically speaking, *Pagliacci* represents one of the sharpest compositional turnarounds in the history of opera. Leoncavallo had been writing *Crepusculum*, a trilogy of operas based in Renaissance Italy, when Mascagni's *Cavalleria Rusticana* successfully premiered. *Cavalleria*'s combination of brutal truth and high drama must have blown the composer's mind. Abandoning the ranks of the classicists and post-Wagnerians, Leoncavallo became a leading exponent of *verismo* operas, "slices of life" about real people in unidealized situations. *Pagliacci* was inspired by a real event that took place in a Calabrian village. The court case was judged by Leoncavallo's own father.

Pagliacci is, of course, the ideal *verismo*: the fourth wall is broken immediately when Tonio addresses the audience in the Prologue; there are anger, adultery, attempted rape, rage, and revenge galore; and a character is killed in full view of the audience. And when Canio tells the audience at the opera's close that "La commedia è finita!," all theatrical politeness is abandoned. We, the audience, have become witnesses to a crime.

WHO'S WHO

Canio, head of a troupe of strolling players; Pagliaccio in the play (tenor)

Nedda, Canio's wife; Colombina in the play (soprano)

Tonio, a member of the troupe; Taddeo in the play (baritone)

Silvio, a villager, Nedda's lover (baritone)

WHAT'S HAPPENING

Calabrian village, nineteenth century

The Prologue presents Tonio (Taddeo), who warns the opera audience that the passions to come may not be limited to the actors' stage.

In Act I, the villagers welcome the players, and spirits are high all around—even though Canio warns that to joke about infidelity onstage is one thing but real-life cuckoldry is quite another. Later, the hunchbacked Tonio flirts lasciviously with Nedda, but she taunts and curses him and strikes him with a whip. Nedda is clearly unhappy with Canio and has a rendezvous with Silvio, with whom she is in love. Overhearing the lovers, the bitter Tonio tells Canio, but the show must go on.

In Act II, the play is performed. In it, Nedda plays the role of an unfaithful lover, the action of the play mirroring the players' real-life situation, and the increasingly demented Canio stabs both Nedda and Silvio. Finally, hysterical, he tells the audience, "The comedy is over."

FAR MORIRE

Act I: The Prologue is sung by Tonio in front of the curtain: it is not only a baritone showcase but a perfect scene setter; he tells us what is about to take place. Canio's scene "Un tal gioco," in which he warns that if what happens onstage were to happen in real life, there would be real ugliness; we learn how violent he could be in this aria. And, of course, Canio's aria "Vesti la giubba," which is great when sung in the opera but too sappy when done in concert—as it too often is.

Act II: Pagliaccio's outburst and finale, "No, Pagliaccio non son."

Umberto Giordano

Umberto Giordano (1867–1948) wrote thirteen operas; by the middle of the twentieth century he was known for only one: *Andrea Chénier*. Since then only *Fedora* has become a household name among aficionados, while *La Cena delle Beffe*, *Il Re*, *Mala Vita*, and *Siberia* are names vaguely familiar to opera obsessives and the others have disappeared entirely (*Regina Diaz*?). His first work, *Marina*, written when he was twenty, came in sixth out of seventy-three in a competition; his second, *Mala Vita*, was a tough-hearted work about a laborer with tuberculosis who swears to reform a prostitute if he is cured. It premiered in Rome in 1892 and caused an uproar, not all of it pleasant, but went on to be staged in Prague, Vienna, and Berlin. Both *Andrea Chénier* and *Fedora* were great successes, but it is sad to note that every opera thereafter flopped, and he gave up in 1930 and died eighteen years later. A very odd legacy.

Andrea Chénier

Four acts
First performance: Teatro alla Scala, Milan, 1896
Libretto: Luigi Illica

"You have only to find a beautiful melody and build an opera around it," said Giordano, and he seems to have been right. While there's something cornball about this work—the whole setup reeks of melodrama and the characters may talk deep but they aren't particularly—perform it with a star tenor and soprano, make it loud, and give in to its clatter, and it can knock an audience out and leave them screaming for more. As always, the background of the French Revolution is engrossing, and there are at least four of those "beautiful melodies" in the opera—pieces you wish you could hear again, immediately.

In 1888, the music publisher Edoardo Sonzogno created a competition for composers of one-act operas. Mascagni's *Cavalleria Rusticana* was the winner, but Umberto Giordano, another entrant, showed enough promise for Sonzogno to commission a second work from him. Though Giordano's subsequent two tries were flops, Sonzogno stuck by him anyway. With *Andrea Chénier,* he scored a resounding success: at the premiere, there were twenty curtain calls for the singers and Giordano. The tenor, particularly, with an aria in each act and two big duets, was applauded, as tenors have been in the title role ever since.

There was a real André Chénier, who, like the fictional one, was a poet and a philosopher; however, the real man was also a revolutionary. The operatic Chénier tries to remain outside the events of the time but gets caught up despite his highfalutin belief in the power of love. Melodramatic hooey, but the singing for soprano and tenor together, yelling their heads off (all puns intended), makes it worth it.

Maddalena's emotionally over-the-top third-act aria, "La mamma morta," is a nervous breakdown in song. As she recalls seeing her mother die at the hands of the revolutionaries, Maddalena is clearly raving and having visions—and the right singer will bring you to the edge of madness yourself. This is also the aria that so moves Tom Hanks's dying character in the film *Philadelphia*. The recording used in that film is by Maria Callas and will put you through the emotional wringer.

Here is some of the (translated) text:

> They killed my mother in the doorway of my room.
> She died and saved me.
> I looked at it! Where I was born was on fire!
> I was alone and surrounded by nothingness.
> It was then, in my grief, that love came to me
> And murmured in a sweet, melodious voice
> You must live! I am life itself!

I will walk with you and be your support! Smile and hope!
  I'm love itself!
Is all around you blood and mire? I am divine! I can make
  you forget!
I am the god who descends to Earth
  from the empyrean and makes this world a paradise! Ah!
I am love, love, love
And the angel approaches, kisses me, and in that kiss is
  death!
The moribund body is my body, so take it.
I have already died like that!

WHO'S WHO

Andrea Chénier, a poet (tenor)
Maddalena de Coigny, a wealthy aristocrat who falls for
  Chénier (soprano)
Carlo Gérard, the Countess de Coigny's servant; later a
  revolutionary (baritone)

WHAT'S HAPPENING

Paris in the time of the French Revolution

In Act I, at a fancy-dress soiree given by the Countess de Coigny,
Chénier recites his work for her daughter, Maddalena, decrying
man's misery in contrast to nature's beauty. Gérard, a servant fed
up with his lot (and secretly desiring Maddalena), drags a band
of beggars into the party, but the noble guests are oblivious of the
danger ahead.

Act II brings the Revolution into full swing—with Gérard as one of its leaders. Chénier and Maddalena reunite, but he is wanted as a counterrevolutionary. A spy tracks him down, but Gérard warns him in time.

In Act III, Gérard's lust for Maddalena has been rekindled, but his patriotic zeal and her refusal to give in to his advances combine to make him sign an indictment against Chénier. Maddalena offers herself to Gérard, who then tells the council the charges were false, but they are both too late and Chénier is sentenced to death.

In Act IV, at the prison, Maddalena changes places with a condemned woman; she goes with Chénier to the guillotine.

FAR MORIRE

Act I: Chénier's aria "Un dì all'azzurro spazio" is a rousing poem to injustice with huge, tenorial high notes. Sung properly, this impassioned plea for love and justice makes the hair on your neck stand up. It's what opera (and great tenors) is about.

Act II: Chénier and Maddalena's duet "Ecco l'altare . . . Eravate possente . . . Ora soave": a love duet both tender and passionate, showstopping in its buildup.

Act III: Gérard's aria "Nemico della patria"; Maddalena's aria "La mamma morta," described above.

Act IV: Chénier's gentle, hopeless aria "Come un bel dì di maggio"; the final duet, "Vicino a te," with voices, orchestra, and emotions at fever pitch.

Giacomo Puccini

If you like gorgeous, sublimely singable, memorable melodies, Giacomo Puccini (1858–1924) is your man. In our age, the composer's tunes would probably be permanently lodged in the Top 40—and he might live in Nashville. But happily, the maestro was, instead, born in nineteenth-century Tuscany. Puccini's family had been musicians and composers for generations, so it was no surprise that he never considered another calling. After studying with (among others) Ponchielli, the young man quickly found his place on the opera stage. In a shockingly brief twenty-year span, he amassed a body of work that remains unrivaled for sheer *italiano* beauty, each of which features a major soprano role: *Manon Lescaut, La Bohème, Tosca, Madama Butterfly,* and *La Fanciulla del West* (to name a few). A heavy smoker (lung cancer killed him) and a womanizer (his wife tormented a local girl to suicide by accusing her of having had an affair with Giacomo; a postmortem autopsy found the girl to be a virgin), he was (and is) nevertheless revered as a national hero, but his work was also enormously popular in his lifetime abroad. His arias—and high spots—really don't need much analysis: their straightforward emotionality and nonstilted situations are so clear that they go straight to the pleasure center.

Manon Lescaut

Four acts

First performance: Teatro Regio, Turin, 1893

**Libretto: Ruggero Leoncavallo, Marco Praga, Domenico Oliva,
Luigi Illica, Giuseppe Giacosa, Giulio Ricordi, and the composer**

"Massenet feels it like a Frenchman, with the powder and the minuets. I shall tell it as an Italian, with desperate passion." So announced Giacomo Puccini when he decided that he would set the subject of Abbé Prévost's novel to music so soon after the enormous success of Jules Massenet's *Manon*. Of course, having hurled down the gauntlet, Puccini needed a superb libretto. You might think that the story—love waylays a young woman en route to the convent; her piety quickly transforms into pleasure seeking, and her fickleness leads to unhappiness for everyone—would write itself, but you'd be wrong. The first librettist was Puccini's composer friend (and later rival—see entry for *La Bohème*) Ruggero Leoncavallo; then came the novelist Marco Praga, followed by the poet Domenico Oliva. However, none of these options pleased Giulio Ricordi, Puccini's publisher, who hired Giuseppe Giacosa and then, finally, Luigi Illica. All five writers never quite turned out a literary masterpiece, but Puccini's music makes up for any weaknesses in the libretto. Indeed, it was his first great success, brimming over with enthusiasm and easy, memorable tunes. When the opera was performed in London, George Bernard Shaw wrote that Puccini was "more like the heir to Verdi than any of his rivals."

WHO'S WHO

Manon Lescaut (soprano)
Chevalier des Grieux (tenor)
Lescaut, Manon's brother (baritone)
Geronte de Ravoir, treasurer-general, Manon's wealthy elderly suitor (bass)

WHAT'S HAPPENING

France, second half of the eighteenth century

In Act I, Manon and her brother stop at an inn, awaiting a carriage that will take her on to her convent. She catches the eye of des Grieux, who learns that old Geronte plans to abduct her. He convinces her to run away with him instead.

In Act II, in Paris, Manon is ensconced with the rich Geronte but carrying on with des Grieux. She is well cared for but bored, and when des Grieux appears, she begs his forgiveness and they declare their passion for each other. As they are about to leave together, Geronte has Manon arrested as a harlot and a thief.

In Act III, at Le Havre, Lescaut and des Grieux hope to rescue Manon before she is deported to America. They almost succeed, but guards suddenly surround them. The ship's captain takes pity on des Grieux and allows him to come aboard.

Act IV takes the couple to "the plains of Louisiana," where Manon collapses from illness—and self-reproach. She dies in the arms of des Grieux.

FAR MORIRE

Act I: "Donna non vidi mai," des Grieux's instant response to seeing Manon for the first time.

Act II: In Manon's aria "In quelle trine morbide" she sadly muses on how luxurious her life is but how even the silken curtains give off a chill. The duet "Tu, tu, amore? Tu?" features the two lovers who have been separated for a while; their passion is palpable. And later, in des Grieux's aria "Ah, Manon, mi tradisce," he blames her greed for causing them such unhappiness—it is a torrent of bare feeling.

Act III: As Manon is boarding the ship that will take her to exile in America, des Grieux explodes with raw feeling again, in "No! pazzo son! Guardate." This is his last heart-ripping eruption, but it qualifies him as Puccini's most impetuous young lover.

Act IV: Manon's aria "Sola, perduta, abbandonata" ideally expresses her fear and despair; she dies moments after it is finished.

La Bohème (The Bohemian Life)

Four acts
First performance: Teatro Regio, Turin, 1896
Libretto: Luigi Illica and Giuseppe Giacosa

La Bohème is Puccini's most lovable opera. It's easy to see why: the music is gorgeous, there are no villains, and the characters are easy to like and relate to. But Ruggero Leoncavallo, the composer of Pagliacci, did not love La Bohème, and he had a very good reason. One afternoon in March 1893, the two composers, who were friendly acquaintances and fans of each other's work, met in a café. Puccini mentioned that he was at work on an adaptation of *Scènes de la vie de bohème*, the then-popular collection of stories by Henri Murger set in the Latin Quarter of Paris in the 1840s, that featured the lives, loves, and ultimately tragic fates of four struggling artists. Furious, Leoncavallo announced that he, too, was writing a version of the tale. The daily papers quickly picked up the story (yes, this was when a rivalry between two opera composers was tabloid-worthy), and Puccini was quoted as saying that Leoncavallo could go ahead and write his *Bohème*—but he wouldn't be deterred. The outcome is well known: Leoncavallo's piece appeared a year after Puccini's and has rarely been more than a curiosity. For millions of opera lovers, attending Puccini's *La Bohème* is the ultimate operatic experience. It is so straightforward—the characters' conversations have a rhythm to them that is absolutely natural and not at all "operatic"—that it also is useful as a first opera for beginners. Its art is so effortless that it takes one listen to love it and many to realize how superb a construction it is. By the way, everyone cries at the end, so don't be embarrassed. I'm not kidding.

WHO'S WHO

Rodolfo, a poet (tenor)
Marcello, a painter (baritone)
Colline, a philosopher (bass)
Schaunard, a musician (baritone)
Mimì, a seamstress (soprano)
Musetta, a singer (soprano)

The cast of La Bohème *in Berlin during Act II. The spontaneity is outdone only by the amazingly ugly clothing—if these are wacky bohemians, the rest of society must look like the kaiser.*

WHAT'S HAPPENING

Latin Quarter of Paris and environs, about 1830

Act I: Rodolfo, who lives with three friends in a garret, meets and falls in love with Mimì, a frail seamstress who lives on the floor below.

In Act II, Mimì joins the men for Christmas Eve dinner at a café. As she responds to admiring glances, Rodolfo shows the first signs that he is a jealous lover. Marcello is no stranger to the condition, having spotted his former sweetheart, Musetta, dining nearby with a wealthy old man. She refocuses her charms on Marcello, and they reunite.

By Act III, Mimì's health has worsened; almost worse, Rodolfo's jealousy is tearing them apart. Mimì overhears him tell Marcello that she is a flirt, though he then goes on to confess his real fear: that she is dying and beyond his help. Shocked, she sees that she and her poet must part. After an argument, Musetta and Marcello make the same decision.

Back in the garret in Act IV, the artist friends mask their troubles with jokes and high jinks. Musetta suddenly appears, bringing Mimì for her final farewell. When she dies, Rodolfo will not believe it until he sees the pain on the others' faces. He can only cry out her name as the curtain falls.

FAR MORIRE

Act I: Rodolfo's and Mimì's rhapsodic arias of introduction, "Che gelida manina" and "Mi chiamano Mimì"; the duet that ends the act, "O soave fanciulla." Rarely do fifteen minutes tell us so much about anyone. Each character's aria is autobiographical, but it is the music that carries them along—Rodolfo's matter-of-fact phrasing as he describes that he's a poet and the total change of mood when he describes what gives him hope; Mimì's utter simplicity in describing how she embroiders and the euphoric blossoming of her vocal line when she describes the outdoors. The brief final duet (with interruptions from Rodolfo's friends downstairs) defines young love, with its soaring phrases, flirtatious asides, and stunning ascent to high C at its close.

Act II: Musetta's enticing "Waltz Song" ("Quando m'en vo'")

and the ensemble that follows it, joining all of the cast members in harmony—and friendship.

Act III: The sensitive duet between Mimì and Marcello; Mimì's farewell, "Donde lieta uscì," as sad and earnest as anything in opera; the duet in which Mimì and Rodolfo agree to part when spring arrives.

Act IV: "O Mimì, tu più non torni," a duet for Marcello and Rodolfo in which they don't sing to each other but express their feelings about their missing girlfriends introspectively; the final ten minutes of the opera, after Mimì and Rodolfo are left alone.

Tosca

Three acts
First performance: Teatro Costanzi, Rome, 1900
Libretto: Luigi Illica and Giuseppe Giacosa

Tosca has been called "a shabby little shocker," and, indeed, the opera's realism is gritty and cold-blooded enough to make responsible parents keep their children at home—not that it's possible to shock children anymore. The three opening chords are so fierce that we know that no joy is to be found here; they are heard again when the evil Scarpia arrives on the scene. Tosca is a singer, a prima donna whose passions run high, especially for her lover, the high-minded Cavaradossi. Her tempestuous nature makes her an easy mark for the diabolical chief of police, Scarpia. The outcome seems to point toward happiness, but, of course, tragedy befalls.

Puccini was scrupulous about *Tosca*'s musical authenticity. For the "Te Deum" that closes Act I, the composer consulted a priest about the correct plainsong melody. Further, a musician in the Vatican informed him of the exact pitch of the bell of Saint Peter's and the words of the Roman shepherd boy's Act III song were written to fit by a Roman poet. Finally, Puccini himself went to Rome to hear what the matin bells sounded like from the top of the Castel Sant'Angelo, where the opera's final act takes place. In other words, *Tosca* may be shocking, but its composition was anything but shabby, evoking Rome and the Church as well as individual passions.

WHO'S WHO

Mario Cavaradossi, a painter (tenor)
Floria Tosca, a singer (soprano)
Baron Scarpia, the chief of police (baritone)
Cesare Angelotti, a political prisoner (bass)

WHAT'S HAPPENING

Rome, 1800

Act I opens in the Church of Sant'Andrea della Valle, where Mario Cavaradossi is painting a mural. When Angelotti dashes onto the scene, having escaped from prison, Cavaradossi offers to hide him in a well in his garden. Tosca makes her entrance, misinterpreting her lover's secrecy for an intrigue with Angelotti's sister. Scarpia enters, suspicious, followed by Tosca, looking for

Mario again. Feeding her suspicions, Scarpia hopes for information—and, eventually, for Tosca herself.

In Act II, Scarpia arrests Cavaradossi, even though the police have found no evidence of his treason. Tosca appears, and Cavaradossi tells her the truth—where Angelotti is hiding—before he is taken away to be tortured. Forced to listen to her lover's screams, Tosca breaks down and tells Scarpia all he needs for a conviction. After Scarpia sends Cavaradossi off to await execution, he offers to arrange a mock firing squad in exchange for Tosca's favors. She agrees, but, as soon as he has written out the orders, she stabs him.

"Scarpia, we will meet before God!" Tosca hollers on a high B flat just before she leaps to her death. Her dead boyfriend lies in the foreground, oblivious as to whether or not she makes the note.

Act III reveals Cavaradossi in jail, bravely facing his fate. Tosca rushes in and tells him that the execution will be only a pretense. With a happy heart, he takes his place atop the castle, but the firing squad means business after all. Scarpia's evil has lived on after him, and Tosca leaps off the parapet, following Cavaradossi in death.

FAR MORIRE

Act I: Cavaradossi's aria "Recondita armonia"; the closing "Te Deum" for Scarpia and chorus, with the final spine-chilling line from Scarpia: "O Tosca—you make me forget God!"

Act II: Tosca's confrontation with Scarpia, a tense, nasty battle of wills, leading up to her aria "Vissi d'arte," in which she cries out that she has always lived for art and been a good person— why, she asks, is God paying her back with such torment?

Act III: Cavaradossi's aria "E lucevan le stelle," as he recalls the night he and Tosca were first together and in love. This tenor aria, like Rodolfo's in the first act of *La Bohème* and "Nessun dorma" (in *Turandot*, see below), never fails to rouse an audience.

Madama Butterfly
Three acts
First performance (in two acts): Teatro alla Scala, Milan, 1904
Libretto: Giuseppe Giacosa and Luigi Illica

This is the saddest opera in the standard repertoire. A young girl gives up everything for the man who promises her the world.

When that promise proves false, she chooses death over hopelessness and dishonor. Our heroine is only fifteen at the opera's start and eighteen when she dies; her hope—and then hopelessness—is so vividly depicted and her melodies so beautiful that they get us right in the gut. It's a sure thing.

The opening night of *Madama Butterfly*, however, was one of the greatest fiascos in the history of opera. The entire second act was barely audible through the booing, whistles, laughter, and catcalls of the audience, and the press savaged the piece. Puccini, then at the height of his fame, immediately withdrew it and began revisions. He shortened the first act, omitting much tedious local color in the early wedding scene (Butterfly's uncle, Yakuside, was seen to get drunk), and divided the almost ninety-minute second act—cripplingly long for an Italian audience—in two. Finally, he added a brief but beautiful aria for the tenor ("Addio, fiorito asil"), who otherwise was practically silent in the last act, and shortened and refocused the Butterfly-Kate-Pinkerton scene (it was originally Kate who asked for Butterfly's child). Three months later, the revised *Butterfly* was a resounding success (though Puccini made further revisions until 1906). Nowadays, it is impossible to imagine an operatic world without Puccini's sad geisha.

Incidentally, aiming for verisimilitude, as he did with the "Te Deum" and bells in Tosca, Puccini uses a traditional Japanese melody to open the opera and at one point has Pinkerton sing the words "America forever" right after the brass intones part of "The Star-Spangled Banner."

WHO'S WHO

Cio-Cio-San, or Madama Butterfly (soprano)
B. F. Pinkerton, U.S. Navy lieutenant (tenor)
Sharpless, U.S. consul (baritone)
The Bonze, Butterfly's uncle (bass)
Suzuki, her maid (mezzo-soprano)
Kate, Pinkerton's American wife (mezzo-soprano)

WHAT'S HAPPENING

Nagasaki, early 1900s

In Act I, Pinkerton, who is about to wed Butterfly, insensitively tells Sharpless how he looks forward to marrying a "real American" wife. Butterfly enters, unaware, with her most precious possessions (including the knife her father used to commit hara-kiri). Just as the wedding ceremony ends, her uncle, the Bonze (a religious figure), insists that her family reject her for renouncing her faith.

When Act II begins, Pinkerton has been away for three years, and Butterfly has had his son. She refuses to believe she has been deserted until Sharpless comes to convince her. She is devastated—but then Pinkerton's ship arrives in the harbor, and she and Suzuki strew the house with cherry blossoms and await his return.

In Act III, Butterfly's joy is short-lived. Pinkerton and Kate, his American wife, have come for the boy, and Butterfly, now futureless, must give him up. Her only course is suicide with her father's knife.

FAR MORIRE

Act I: Butterfly's entrance, "Quanto cielo! . . . Ancora un passo or via," which begins offstage and features Butterfly's voice soaring above those of her friends; the main melody is invariably associated with Butterfly's innocent love and recurs every so often during the opera. The love duet "Viene la sera," a rapturous coming together of the shy-but-pliant Butterfly and the smitten, anxious-for-his-new-bride Pinkerton; an ecstatic love scene that builds and builds.

Act II: Butterfly's aria "Un bel dì," a psychodrama: Butterfly imagines Pinkerton's return—indeed, she lives through it moment by moment; the scene between Butterfly and Sharpless and her breakdown, hysterical at the prospect of returning to her life as a geisha; the lovely cherry blossom duet for Suzuki and Butterfly, "Scuoti quella fronda di ciliegio," with its exotic mingling of voices.

Act III: Pinkerton's impassioned aria "Addio fiorito asil," in which he expresses his regret; Butterfly's death scene, "Con onor muore," a gut-wrenching suicide scene that ends with Pinkerton's racing into the room—too late.

La Fanciulla del West (The Girl of the Golden West)

Three acts
First performance: Metropolitan Opera, New York, 1910
Libretto: Carlo Zangarini and Guelfo Civinini

Set in the Cloudy Mountains of California, *La Fanciulla del West* is a truly Italian salute to the American West. It is also Puccini's least "Puccini-like" opera, relying less on set pieces and catchy melodies than it does on inventive touches. Act I offers Debussy-like, impressionistic orchestration; Act II's "poker scene" finds the soprano and baritone barely singing (so stifling is the tension) against a background of pizzicato double basses; Act III goes out with a whisper, both vocally and orchestrally. Despite these oddities—or perhaps because of them—Maurice Ravel found the score extraordinary and instructed his pupils to study it, and Richard Strauss said he would like to have composed the second act. The audience at the world premiere in New York loved it, too; Puccini was present, Caruso and Emmy Destinn sang, Arturo Toscanini conducted, and there were more than fifty curtain calls at the end. Minnie's vocal line is so difficult—high and fierce at times, with much to sing—that it has become known as "Puccini's Valkyrie." Very few sopranos ever try it.

Fun fact: What spectacularly successful latter-twentieth-century musical's Big Theme was "borrowed" from *La Fanciulla del West*? A broad hint: the first word of the title means "ghost," and the final words are "of the opera."

WHO'S WHO

Minnie, saloon keeper, Bible teacher (soprano)
Dick Johnson, aka the bandit Ramerrez (tenor)
Jack Rance, sheriff (baritone)

WHAT'S HAPPENING

California mining camp during the Gold Rush, 1849–1850

Act I: Dick Johnson, a newcomer, swings his way into the Polka Saloon. Minnie, a heroine who brings out the best in a bunch of rowdy men, has met him briefly before and falls for him on the spot. Sheriff Rance, who wants Minnie for his own, suspects that Dick is really Ramerrez, a bandit on the lam.

In Act II, Johnson/Ramerrez visits Minnie in her cabin, and she discovers his real identity. She tells him to leave, and when he does and the sheriff's posse wounds him, the love-struck Minnie hides him in her loft. Rance discovers him there, but Minnie challenges Rance to a poker game with Johnson as the prize. She cheats and wins; Rance retreats.

However, in Act III, Johnson has been captured anyway. He is about to be hanged when Minnie gallops up, makes the miners realize all she has done for them, and saves Johnson—this time for good—as they ride out of town on their horses.

FAR MORIRE

Once you get over the fact that you are watching a "western" in opera form—the miners in Act I sing "Hello, Minnie!" and ask for "whiskey"—this opera's sophisticated score and, as usual with Puccini, raw emotion take over and will win you over—much to your own surprise.

Act I: Rance's aria "Minnie, dalla mia casa," in which the sheriff tells Minnie how much he loves her and it's clear that she does not reciprocate: Rance may be our villain, but he is capable of great love. "Mister Johnson" is a duet for Minnie and Johnson that ends the act, a tender love duet all the more effective because the individuals' facades are so seemingly tough.

Act II: Johnson's aria "Una parola sola . . . or son sei mesi," a plea for understanding from Minnie for the life he was forced to lead after his bandit father died six months before; the startlingly tense poker scene finale, which ends with Minnie going vocally ballistic and sounding very much like, yes, one of Wagner's Valkyries.

Act III: "Ch'ella mi creda libero" (Please let her think I'm free), Johnson sings as he's about to be hanged; Minnie's whooping entrance and the final ensemble in which she pleads for Johnson's life.

Turandot
Three acts
First performance: Teatro alla Scala, Milan, 1926
Libretto: Giuseppe Adami and Renato Simoni

Turandot was Puccini's last opera, one he did not live to complete. It was completed by the composer Franco Alfano from three dozen pages of sketches Puccini left. The opera is, in many ways, the apotheosis of his art. The surreal rising of the moon in Act I is weirdly impressionistic; the ensemble that closes the act, beginning with Liù's and Calaf's arias and ending with the striking of the gong that will change Calaf's fate, is suspenseful enough to please any fan of *verismo*; the commedia dell'arte trio of Ping, Pang, and Pong in Act II is an ideal comic interlude. Princess Turandot herself is the quintessential cruel beauty—"the ice that gives off fire"—and Liù is a long-suffering woman in love. The title role, though short (she does not sing until Act II), is ferocious—she must sing full voice over a huge orchestra, and most of the high notes are exposed. Many Wagnerian sopranos who have but one role in the Italian repertory have shone in the part: it is a role for the brave. The opera has always been a favorite among Puccini enthusiasts, but the 1990 World Cup, at which Luciano Pavarotti sang the tenor's third-act aria "Nessun dorma," really made it a household word.

In short, *Turandot* is strong, yet absolutely lyrical, the perfect example of what Puccini referred to musically as "striking out on new paths." (As well as the "new," we also see the old Puccini in Liù's music; it could be Mimì's or Manon's.) With the light tunefulness, we get the acme of darkness he had only hinted at in earlier operas, and the abundance of shadows makes the maestro's own untimely death all the more tragic.

WHO'S WHO

Turandot, Princess of Peking (soprano)
Calaf, exiled Prince of Tartary (tenor)
Timur, Calaf's father (bass)
Liù, slave to Timur and Calaf (soprano)

WHAT'S HAPPENING

Peking, legendary times

In Act I, Turandot's most recent suitor is to be executed, having failed to pass the trial-by-riddles. Present for the occasion is Prince Calaf, who catches sight of the princess and declares that he will be the next to try, much to the unhappiness of his father, Timur, and their slave girl, Liù.

He gets his chance in Act II and answers all three questions correctly. But Turandot is so distraught at his success that he poses a riddle of his own: if she can guess his name by morning, he will die as did all the suitors before him.

Act III brings a desperate search for Calaf's name: Turandot has Liù tortured and then watches as the girl kills herself to protect the secret. Calaf reproaches Turandot for her heartlessness, but he goes on to embrace her and to reveal his name. Instead of calling for his execution, she calls out his name—and it is "Love."

FAR MORIRE

Act I: Liù's aria "Signore, ascolta!"; Calaf's aria "Non piangere, Liù." Both arias exemplify the height of Puccini's lyrical gifts, and each requires sensitive singing. The end of Calaf's aria segues right into the act's ensemble finale, which ends with him striking the gong—a sign that he will be the next to be questioned by Turandot.

Act II: Turandot's aria "In questa reggia," the psychological response to her coldness: one of her ancestors was carried away by foreign conquerors and it is her, Turandot's, desire to avenge her. Her resolve is clear in her vocal line—high notes taken in anger as memories of her ancestor's screams; and the riddle scene "Straniero, ascolta!," which builds to a brutal finale as Turandot almost goes mad realizing she may have to give herself to Calaf.

Act III: Calaf's aria "Nessun dorma" is the score's most famous aria due to Pavarotti's World Cup performance, and it deserves its fame. It is a melody of great beauty, an aria full of resolve, with the word "vincerò" set on a grand, tenorial high B—a crowning note for a crowning statement. And Liù's death scene, "Tu che di gel sei cinta," shows her to be not truly one of Puccini's frail women but one whose moral convictions and loyalties are ferocious.

French Opera

DEMONS, GYPSIES, BIBLICAL EPICS

In 1671 the first opera house was built in France; operas prior to that had been lavish displays at court with lots of dancing and elaborate scenery, since King Louis XIV preferred dancing to singing. Plots invariably had some metaphoric relationship to Louis, and after initial runs for royalty, they might be played for the general public. Jean-Baptiste Lully (1632–1687), born in Italy, was given a monopoly on the art form by Louis; great though Lully was, this stunted opera's growth in France (Italian repertory was frequently presented by visiting Italian companies). Not to speak in crude generalities, but the music to French opera tends to be more sugary than that by non-French composers, and, yes, the love for ballet that was so clear at Versailles at the end of the seventeenth century lasted through the end of the nineteenth century. If you go to see a French opera, the odds are that you'll have to sit through lots of dancing, sometimes integrated into the plot, sometimes not. Since most opera companies have poor *corps de ballet*, feel free to take this time to rest your eyes.

Charles Gounod

One look at the daguerreotype photograph of the heavily whiskered, beetle-browed Charles Gounod (1818–1893) reveals a man who lived well and seriously. Always religious (his church music is among his most performed and famous work), Gounod himself believed that the opera stage was the "one road to follow in order to make a name" as a composer. Still, his best-known opera is, of course, *Faust*, the prototypical passion play about a man challenged—and bested—by ultimate evil. He is considered a High French Romantic; his work is lyrical, dramatic, and—to some scholars—(almost) excessively sentimental. In his later years, the composer went back to his first musical love: liturgical works. In addition to his "Ave Maria" and other religious pieces, his opera *Roméo et Juliette* continues to be performed.

Faust
Five acts
First performance: Théâtre-Lyrique, Paris, 1859
Libretto: Jules Barbier and Michel Carré

The Faust legend has fascinated people for centuries. Its origins contain some measure of truth. There actually was a Dr. Faust who lived in Knittingen, Germany, from 1480 to 1540. Known as a magician or sorcerer of sorts, he was mentioned in sermons by German Protestant reformers in the mid-1500s and memorialized in the drama *The Tragical History of Doctor Faustus* by Christopher Marlowe. The story has stayed pretty much the same ever since: Faust sells his soul to the Devil for a two-pronged payoff: a return to youth and the love of the innocent Marguerite. No good can come from this evil plan, but there is at least some heavenly intervention at the very end.

After Marlowe, the legend of Man against Ultimate Evil really solidified when Johann Wolfgang von Goethe, Paul Valéry, and Thomas Mann each wrote his own version of his tale, and Rembrandt and Eugène Delacroix depicted him in their work. Faust also captured the imagination of a variety of composers, including Franz Schubert, Hector Berlioz, Franz Liszt, Arrigo Boito, Louis Spohr, Richard Wagner, Gustav Mahler, and Ferruccio Busoni. Gounod's opera, however, is the most popular incarnation. The story remains riveting because of the alluring and appalling character of Doctor Faust himself. In the Reformation days of hellfire and brimstone, this man was willing to risk his soul. Even now, we find his story and self-immolating choice a fascinating morality play.

WHO'S WHO

Faust, an aged philosopher (tenor)
Méphistophélès (bass)
Marguerite (soprano)
Valentin, Marguerite's brother (baritone)

WHAT'S HAPPENING

Germany, sixteenth century

In Act I, the aging Faust is ripe for Méphistophélès, who offers his tempting contract. As soon as Faust signs it, he is young again, and he leaves with the Devil to snare Marguerite.

The fourth-act duel scene from Faust, *fixed from the start. If you see three men dressed like this in your town, there's probably an interesting parade somewhere nearby.*

In Acts II and III, Marguerite falls into the arms of Faust, unable to resist the jewels or the spell Méphistophélès produces.

By Act IV, Faust has deserted her, even though she is carrying his child. Overcome with shame, she enters a church to repent. Now after her soul as well, Méphistophélès sends a chorus of demons to vie with the choir. Faust duels with Marguerite's outraged brother, Valentin, who dies by the lost soul's fiendishly guided sword.

In Act V, in the midst of bacchanalian revels, Faust sees a vision of Marguerite, imprisoned for the murder of her child. He goes to her, accompanied, as ever, by Méphistophélès. Seeing them together, she finally understands their evil complicity and calls on angels to save her. They bear her toward Heaven as she dies.

LES PETITES MORTS

Act I: Faust and Méphistophélès's duet "A moi les plaisirs!," a rousing duet of friendship and excitement, sung after the Devil restores Faust's youth. Faust's enthusiasm is well matched by Méphistophélès's, though for very different reasons.

Act II: Valentin's aria "Avant de quitter ces lieux" in which he prepares to go off to battle with the good-luck medallion Marguerite has given him—the aria is rightly well known and shows the high baritone voice and elegant French style at their best; Méphistophélès's jeering aria "Le veau d'or" (The Golden Calf)—designed to mock the religious townspeople, it is a stirring piece of blasphemy and showcases the bass voice at its most booming.

Act III: Faust's aria "Salut! Demeure," certainly in the running for French opera's most gorgeous tenor aria, with its ascent to high C at the end; Marguerite's "Jewel Song," in which the innocent girl wonders who left her the lovely box of jewels and revels in their beauty—the aria is full of trills and upward runs designed to express Marguerite's delight and surprise. Marguerite and Faust's lengthy duet "Il se fait tard!" is both seductive and sincere; the listener forgets the sinister plotting surrounding the love affair.

Act IV: The church scene: Marguerite, chorus, Méphistophélès. This remarkable scene, which begins with an organ solo, finds Marguerite in a church praying, but with every phrase she sees and hears Méphistophélès behind her, reminding her of her guilt, and a chorus of invisible fiends calls for her damnation: a strangely effective and terrifying scene.

Act V: The prison-scene duet "Oui, c'est moi, je t'aime!" for Marguerite and Faust; the stirring, if brief, final trio with Méphistophélès, "Alerte! Alerte! . . . Anges purs," in which Marguerite prays for forgiveness, the music modulating upward toward the heavens.

Georges Bizet

Georges Bizet (1838–1875) is one of those composers who is known primarily for a single piece—in his case *Carmen*, the story of a doomed-yet-hot cigarette-factory-worker-slash-smuggler and her crazed soldier-boy lover. "The Toreador Song" and "Habanera" are probably two of the most recognizable tunes in the world. However, Bizet also wrote *The Pearl Fishers*, an "exotic"

CALVE AS CARMEN

Emma Calvé as Carmen, cigarette in place, wearing a pretty fancy dress for a factory worker. The most famous French opera singer of her era, she is said to have been the greatest interpreter of Carmen ever to hit the stage. She was also rumored to be a Cathar, a member of an anti-Catholic secret medieval religious sect that believed in two gods, a God of Good and a God of Evil. That has nothing to do with opera, but it certainly is "operatic."

opera set in Ceylon (the subject and locale no doubt appealed to the midcentury dream of the mysterious Orient), which contains at least a pair of excerpts that are as beautiful as they are memorable. His Symphony in C is a Romantic masterpiece—lush, exciting, and sexy. It further astonishes because the composer wrote it as a school assignment when he was only seventeen. This probably seemed normal to his schoolmates at the Paris Conservatory, where Bizet's virtuosity was soon the stuff of awe and legend. Though his work did not always receive the critical acclaim it deserved, he was deeply admired by his musical colleagues, including Claude Debussy and Johannes Brahms. Tragically, he did not live to see his work celebrated. In a fate more suited to an Italian operatic heroine, he caught a chill after swimming one summer afternoon and died, at thirty-seven years of age.

Carmen
Four acts
First performance: Opéra-Comique, Paris, 1875
Libretto: Henri Meilhac and Ludovic Halévy

Don José, a young soldier on duty in Seville, has no reason not to believe he will return to his village, his devoted mother, and his intended bride, Micaëla. But he meets the beautiful and restless Carmen, she tosses him a bloodred flower, and all innocence disappears in a cloud of Gypsy smoke.

When *Carmen* first appeared more than a century and a quarter ago, it sent shock waves through decent society everywhere.

Women were fighting and smoking onstage, and the heroine was the most brazen and unrepentantly sexual creature audiences had ever seen. Subscribing to no accepted social norms, Carmen sings about herself, "Libre elle est née, et libre elle mourra!" (She was born free and will die free!). By today's standards, Carmen seems a free-spirited young woman with a somewhat dubious taste in boyfriends. José, however, is obviously a sexually repressed lunatic who had never been out of the clutches of his mother and virginal girlfriend, filled with angers and frustrations just waiting to explode. Ripped from today's high school headlines.

WHO'S WHO

Carmen, a Gypsy (soprano or mezzo-soprano)
Micaëla, a peasant girl (soprano)
Don José, a soldier (tenor)
Escamillo, a toreador (bass-baritone)

WHAT'S HAPPENING

Seville, Spain, about 1820

Act I opens with Carmen in a crowd of cigarette-factory girls, besotting every soldier she passes except for Don José, whose indifference spurs her on to cast her spell on him. When she becomes his prisoner following a factory brawl, she tosses a flower at him; he allows her to escape and goes to prison himself.

In Act II, while waiting for Don José's release, Carmen flirts with the toreador Escamillo. She rejects him, but only for the moment. When Don José appears, she dances sensually for him but then mocks and teases him when he says he must return to his barracks. She makes him join her band of smugglers.

At their camp, in Act III, Don José faces two unexpected visitors: Escamillo, who declares himself to be Carmen's new lover, and Micaëla, who has come to take him to his dying mother.

Act IV brings Don José back to Seville to confront Carmen. But she now belongs to Escamillo, turning her back on José's desperate pleas. He pulls a knife. He is a slave to passion and revenge; his release can come only with her death.

LES PETITES MORTS

Act I: Carmen's habañera "L'amour est un oiseau rebelle," an enticing song that explains her philosophy of romance: "Love is like a rebellious bird that will not listen to law. . . . If you want me I don't want you; if I love you, be careful." She's not kidding—she is passionate and changeable. And in her seguidilla, another hip-swinging number she sings while handcuffed and alone with José, she implies doing all sorts of things with him in a place just outside the city.

Act II: The opening Gypsy song, sung and danced by Carmen and all of her friends, a number that escalates in tempo and mounts in volume and abandon as it goes on, ending in an orgasmic collapse, tambourine rattling. Then come Escamillo's "Toreador Song," which, though a bore, really does define this boastful dope, and Don José's "Flower Song" ("La fleur que tu m'avais jetée"), in which he tells Carmen that the flower she tossed him gave him hope while he was in jail and expresses his love for her. (Note that this aria is crafted so superbly that no phrase is ever repeated—there's no "refrain" or "chorus"; each line is a different thought and buildup of feeling.)

Act III: Carmen's "Card Trio" with her two friends: she tells her own fortune with cards, and the result always comes up the same: death. This is a dark, dark solo for Carmen, with her friends' jolly responses very pointed.

Act IV: The opera's final twelve minutes (the whole last act is only twenty minutes long) has José confronting Carmen outside the bullring. He grovels, weeps—indeed, falls apart in front of her—and she expresses more and more scorn. He finally stabs her; she sees it as her fate. Not that it wasn't expected, but it's a shattering scene.

Camille Saint-Saëns

Born in Paris, Camille Saint-Saëns (1835–1921) was a child prodigy both on the piano and as a composer. He made his professional debut in Paris at age ten playing concertos by Beethoven and Mozart; as an encore he agreed to play any of Beethoven's thirty-two piano sonatas from memory. By all accounts a generally brilliant man, Saint-Saëns included among his close friends Franz Lizst, Hector Berlioz, and Gabriel Fauré (who started out as his student). He was a fan of what could then be termed "new music," such as the "shocking" work of Wagner, but his music has an exquisite French reserve and elegance; he once said that he composed music "as an apple tree produces apples." He remained both popular and active throughout his life, composing many works that are now in the standard orchestral repertoire: *Carnival of the Animals* and his Cello Concerto in A Minor, as well as several works for the organ.

Samson et Dalila

Three acts
First performance: Hoftheater, Weimar, 1877
Libretto: Ferdinand Lemaire

In *Samson et Dalila*, Saint-Saëns and Lemaire (who happened also to be an in-law of the composer) decided to concentrate on the less obviously savage aspects of the famous Old Testament story. Rather than depicting the epic sections of the book of Judges chapter, such as Samson's winning duel with a lion or his slaying of a thousand Philistines with the jawbone of an ass, Lemaire concentrated on the character of Dalila. With the Bible relegated to backdrop, we find in this piece an exquisitely perverse romance. Our arch seductress manipulates the plot with her intensity (and beautiful melodies), though her motivations are less political than sensual. And one can say the same for Samson: these two become, in fact, a perfectly matched couple. That is, until Dalila decides to destroy him.

WHO'S WHO

Dalila, a Philistine (mezzo-soprano)
Samson, leader of the Hebrews (tenor)
High Priest (baritone)

WHAT'S HAPPENING

Gaza (Palestine), biblical time

In Act I, Samson rouses his despairing people to action and leads them to victory against their oppressors, slaying the Satrap of Gaza and scattering the Philistines into the hills. Among the defeated is Dalila, who returns to congratulate her conqueror and former lover.

Samson, in spite of himself, is mesmerized by her charms and, in Act II, appears at her house. Although he has planned to tell her farewell, she wins out and entraps him. Overcome by passion, Samson reveals that his hair holds the secret of his power, and Dalila is triumphant.

In Act III, Samson, shorn (and blinded for good measure), lies in a dungeon, enduring the taunts of Dalila, his captors, his own people, and, most of all, his conscience. Later, as the Philistines' scornful revelry reaches fever pitch, he regains enough strength to pull down the temple and crush them all—including himself.

LES PETITES MORTS

Act I: Samson and chorus: "Arrêtez, ô mes frères!," a stirring pep talk that Samson gives to his people; Dalila's aria "Printemps qui commence," a quiet, reserved, amazingly sensual aria in which she entrances Samson with her sadness and longing.

Act II: Samson and Dalila's scene "En ces lieux, malgré moi . . . Mon coeur s'ouvre à ta voix." Samson enters knowing he is making a mistake by coming to see Dalila, but he can't help himself. She cajoles and seduces him more overtly than in

The British contralto Edna Thornton as Dalila. Though she is almost completely forgotten today, her few extant recordings exhibit a huge, matronly voice that would have had Samson running in the other direction if her dress and the nutso look in her eyes hadn't already scared him half to death.

her first-act aria: in "Mon coeur s'ouvre," Saint-Saëns's accompaniment is torrid and sultry; the text is all sexual metaphor (flowers opening; slow arrows, and so on), and the aria is pure velvet. "Fill me with ecstasy," she repeats over and over again. It's amazing that he doesn't cut his own hair.

Jacques Offenbach

Jacques Offenbach (1819–1880) was born in Germany but moved to France in his teens to attend the Paris Conservatory as a cellist. He soon established himself as both a virtuoso player and a promising young composer. However, the City of Light was not such a congenial place in the early to mid-1800s, as revolutionary upheaval made violence rampant. Too often, Offenbach was a victim of either anti-French or anti-German sentiments in whichever country he chose to settle in at whatever particular political moment. However, this never stopped his composing operettas and songs. As a parodist, his targets were often unhappy about his "light" critiques. Even so, Offenbach remained enormously popular throughout his life, touring Europe and America as a conductor of his own work. With such a sharp sense of humor, it might please the composer to know that at least one of his melodies has stayed alive in countless versions, though far from its original context: we know it as "The Cancan Song" (if you picture chorus girls high-kicking with lots of petticoats, you'll remember the melody) but it is really from Offenbach's comic operetta *Orpheus in the Underworld*.

Les Contes d'Hoffmann
(The Tales of Hoffmann)

Prologue, three acts, and Epilogue
First performance: Opéra-Comique, Paris, 1881
Libretto: Jules Barbier and Michel Carré, based on stories by the
poet E. T. A. Hoffmann

We are presented with the hypersensitive, probably drunken poet Hoffmann regaling his friends with three stories of lost love, each tale also being a poetic metaphor for a stage in Hoffmann's search for Art. Doomed love, sex and death, art, desire, self-delusion, evil incarnate, magic, cruelty for its own sake, paranoia: set most of it to memorable, deceptively merry, or tuneful music and you'll have the paradox that is Offenbach's *Les Contes d'Hoffmann*. Regardless of what version of the opera is being used—and remarkably, in the 1970s more than 1,200 previously unknown pages from many stages of the work's composition were discovered, joined in 1984 by 350 more—these themes remain the same. So it doesn't matter how big a role the Muse has or whether the Giulietta act comes before the Antonia act; everywhere Hoffmann goes, death is present. His three loves spell death: Olympia was never alive to begin with, Antonia is doomed to death if she does the one thing she loves to do (sing), and Giulietta is the bringer of death. And the four villains are working toward Hoffmann's spiritual death. There are recordings available of at least four versions, and the opera keeps changing as pieces are added and subtracted. Because Offenbach died without leaving a "finished" opera, "helpers" were adding music from other Offenbach works as early as 1904: Dapertutto's aria "Scintille, diamant" is from the composer's *Le Voyage dans la Lune*, and the famous septet "Hélas, mon coeur" is rumored to have been composed by the almost unknown André Bloch. No less than Gustav Mahler omitted the Prologue and Epilogue when he conducted the work in Vienna. And the famous barcarolle that opens the Venice act? Borrowed by Offenbach from his own earlier opera *Les Fées du Rhin*!

WHO'S WHO

It was once customary for all of Hoffmann's loves to be sung by the same soprano and his nemeses to be sung by the same bass-baritone, but the opera is rarely performed that way today.

Hoffmann, a poet (tenor)

Nicklausse, Hoffmann's companion (mezzo-soprano)

Stella, a prima donna (soprano)

Olympia, a mechanical doll (soprano)

Giulietta, a courtesan (soprano)

Antonia, a young woman (soprano)

Lindorf, a councilor of Nuremberg (bass-baritone)

Coppélius, Hoffmann's rival (bass-baritone)

Dr. Miracle, a sorcerer (bass-baritone)

Dapertutto, a magician (bass-baritone)

Spalanzani, an inventor (tenor)

WHAT'S HAPPENING

Nuremberg, nineteenth century

In the Prologue, Hoffmann enters a tavern next to an opera house to wait for Stella, an opera singer whom he loves. The entrance of Lindorf, who also loves Stella, reminds Hoffmann of old loves and old rivals, and his student friends urge him to tell his stories.

In Act I, at the home of the inventor Spalanzani, Hoffmann is fooled into believing that Olympia, a doll, is real, until she is torn apart by Coppélius, who helped invent her but was not paid, leaving Hoffmann heartbroken and ridiculed.

Act II, which takes place in Venice, has either of two endings following Giulietta's "theft" (engineered by the sinister Dapertutto) of Hoffmann's reflection: in one, she drinks poison intended for Hoffmann and dies; in the other, she is carried off in a gondola by an admirer.

In Act III, Antonia, a young recluse living in Munich with her father, must never sing, lest she follow in the footsteps of her mother, a mezzo-soprano who sang herself to death. Hoffmann can't keep her from her fate at the hands of Dr. Miracle and therefore loses his third love.

Finally, there is an Epilogue: Back at the tavern, Hoffmann is both downhearted and drunk. Stella arrives, finds him incoherent, and exits with Lindorf. Hoffmann forswears women in favor of his Muse.

LES PETITES MORTS

Prologue: Hoffmann's song with chorus, "Il était une fois à la cour d'Eisenach," is just a little ditty about a dwarf Hoffmann agrees to sing for his friends, but in the middle of it, he goes into a sort of trance and begins describing his beloved's face. It's as fascinating and beautiful as it is weird, and it lets us know that Hoffmann, well, has issues.

Act I: Hoffmann's "Ah! vivre deux!," a sensitive expression of love for Olympia, whom he has just seen; Olympia's song "Les oiseaux dans la charmille," a coloratura showpiece with mechanical-sounding staccati and high notes. Twice Olympia's spring winds down and has to be cranked up; Hoffmann never notices.

Act II: The introductory barcarolle is a languorous duet for two women as they glide down the Grand Canal in Venice on a gondola; Dapertutto's aria "Scintille, diamant," a wicked, melodious song to the diamond he will use to bribe Giulietta into stealing Hoffmann's soul; Hoffmann's euphoric aria "O Dieu! de quelle ivresse," in which he is clearly overwhelmed by Giulietta, his vocal line climbing higher and higher.

Act III: Antonia's aria "Elle a fui, la tourterelle," a sad song that exhausts her; Hoffmann and Antonia's duet "C'est une chanson d'amour," wherein Hoffmann tries to convince Antonia not to sing anymore—a duet so lovely that what it is about is perverse in the extreme; the trio "Ta mère? Oses-tu l'invoquer?" with Dr. Miracle, Antonia, and the voice of Antonia's mother. Dr. Miracle plays the violin, and Antonia hallucinates her mother's voice prompting her to sing louder and higher, to panic pitch. At its close, she collapses.

Russian Opera

CHORUSES, NATIONALISM, AND TCHAIKOVSKY

Opera came to Russia in the 1730s, again from Italy and, as usual, to entertain royalty and the aristocracy. Some of the finest composers of their time (including Giovanni Paisiello and Domenico Cimarosa) went to Moscow and St. Petersburg, but they led Italian operas there. Empress Catherine II sent the now-forgotten Russian composers Maxim Berezovsky and Dmitri Bortniansky to Italy to study with Padre Giovanni Martini (who also taught Mozart) and Baldassare Galuppi, respectively. The first opera written in Russian was Francesco Araja's *Tsefal i Prokris*, staged at St. Petersburg in 1755; no reactions have been documented. But it was not until Mikhail Glinka's two great operas *A Life for the Tsar* (1836) and *Ruslan and Lyudmila* (1842) that Russian opera found its voice: both operas made use of Russian folk melodies and were based in Russian nationalism. To most people, Modest Mussorgsky's *Boris Godunov* is the only Russian opera that matters, but they are wrong; the last half of the nineteenth century and first half of the twentieth witnessed many fine, unique Russian operas. By the way, if it has lots of patriotic and/or religious choruses featuring low men's voices, it's probably Russian.

Modest Mussorgsky

Modest Mussorgsky (1839–1881) is as truly Russian a composer as Puccini is Italian. Bearded and ruddy-cheeked as a peasant, a devotee of his homeland's history and culture, Mussorgsky is renowned for works that are as epic and detailed in scale and form as the works of his literary contemporaries Nikolai Gogol and Alexander Pushkin. Eventually a member of St. Petersburg's bohemian "elite," Mussorgsky, the scion of a wealthy family, began as a piano virtuoso. Like many of his fellow Russian composers (Tchaikovsky in particular), Mussorgsky held a variety of nonmusical jobs. However, he was never less than devoted to his muse, constantly struggling with philosophical definitions of art and expression, rewriting his scores over and over until they received public acceptance. Other than *Boris Godunov*, the composer's best-known works are the glorious symphony favorites *Pictures at an Exhibition* and *Night on Bald Mountain*. Unfortunately, though also in the archetypical Russian/rebellious style of his times, Mussorgsky battled chronic alcoholism for much of his life. In 1881, the by then totally downtrodden composer told a friend that there was "nothing left but begging." He suffered four seizures in a brief period, was hospitalized, and died soon after.

Boris Godunov

Prologue and four acts
First performance: Mariinsky Theatre, St. Petersburg, 1874
Libretto: Written by the composer after Pushkin's play of the same name and Nikolai Karamazin's *History of the Russian State*

This is a chronicle of the rise and fall of one Russian tsar. The way he rose to power—by murdering the infant tsarevich—haunts him throughout his reign and becomes a chief contributor to his downfall.

The machinations of Mussorgsky's Boris make for a wonderful opera plot, but how much of the intrigue is true? Here is some history surrounding the period covered in the opera: after Ivan the Terrible's death, Fyodor, his son by his first wife (he had eight) became tsar. Fyodor was somewhat weak, and his wife's brother, Boris Godunov, soon became the power behind the throne. Ivan's last wife had been sent away with their young son to a monastery, and in 1591 the boy died. The "official investigation" claimed he accidentally stabbed himself in the throat during an epileptic seizure. But there were others who believed that Boris had had him murdered, and still others who felt that the boy escaped the murder attempt. This last theory came to fruition when, in 1603, after Boris had been in power for five

The Russian bass Feodor Chaliapin, one of the earliest of the "naturalist" actors on the opera stage (no "park and bark" from him) as Boris Godunov. As Harold Schonberg wrote, "At the Met he sang the role of Basilio in Rossini's *The Barber of Seville as a vulgar, unctuous, greasy priest, constantly picking his nose and wiping his fingers on his cassock. Audiences were appalled. Defending himself, Chaliapin said in an interview that Basilio 'is a Spanish priest. It is a type I know well. He is not the modern American priest, clean and well-groomed; he is dirty and unkempt, he is a beast, and this is what I make him, a comic beast.'"* Nuff said.

years, a pretender to the throne emerged and made his claim in Poland. Boris died suddenly and mysteriously soon after, and his son was named tsar. This is where the opera ends—but in real life, the son was murdered and the pretender ruled as tsar. However, he, too, was murdered, and Prince Shuisky became tsar! It still isn't known whether or not Boris killed the true heir.

Like *Les Contes d'Hoffmann*, *Boris Godunov* has an incredibly complex performing history. The original version of 1869 was composed of seven scenes, of which Boris appeared in four; the orchestration was relatively sparse, and the harmonies were somewhat unusual. It was rejected by the committee of the imperial theaters. Revised by 1872 to include the "Polish act" (for what was seen as a necessary love interest, not to mention a place for a grand polonaise to be danced) and the Revolution scene, and with cuts elsewhere, it, too, was rejected. Parts of the opera were performed in 1873 (on a program with the second act of Wagner's *Lohengrin*!) in St. Petersburg, but it was not until 1874 that almost all of Mussorgsky's music was played. The public loved it; the critics damned it. By 1882 it had disappeared from the repertory, and it was not heard again until 1896, when Nikolai Rimsky-Korsakov revised and rescored it. This version was played until 1904; Rimsky-Korsakov worked on his own revision from 1906 to 1908, restoring many cuts he had made. Many years later, Dmitri Shostakovich worked on it and created yet another edition, with new orchestration. It is only in the last fifty years that Mussorgsky's original harmonies and settings have gained the respect that they deserve. In whatever form, the mental degeneration of a powerful tsar due to guilt, paranoia, and manipulation is powerfully, shockingly portrayed. This is the greatest of all Russian operas.

WHO'S WHO

Boris Godunov, Tsar of Russia (bass)

Grigory, the pretender Dmitri (tenor)

Pimen, an old monk (bass)

Prince Shuisky (tenor)

Marina Mnishek, a Polish princess (soprano)

Misail, a vagabond (tenor)

Varlaam, a renegade monk (bass)

Rangoni, a Jesuit (bass)

WHAT'S HAPPENING

Russia and Poland, 1598–1605

Prologue: Following the murder of the infant Dmitri, the confused populace urges Boris to take the imperial throne; he hesitantly accepts.

By Act I, Boris has been in power for five years, and times have been hard; even though he has been a diligent ruler, he is blamed for all problems: famine, plague, unrest. At a monastery, the novice Grigory learns from an old monk, Pimen, that the murdered tsarevich would now be his same age. Inspired by this, Grigory leaves the monastery. The second scene of the act takes place at an inn. Grigory and two vagrants, Misail and Varlaam, enter and drink, but the police arrive looking for Grigory, who, upon leaving the monastery, made an unwary comment. He escapes just in time.

By Act II, his role as pretender has been established and Prince Shuisky goes to the tsar's apartments in the Kremlin. He tells Boris about the pretender and then adds to Boris's emotional instability by describing the mystical aura that had surrounded the murdered tsarevich. Could he be, after all, alive? Boris becomes hysterical and collapses.

In Act III, the "Polish act," Princess Marina seeks power for Poland and aims to win the heart of the pretender. A Jesuit, Rangoni, arrives and tells her that when she is on the Russian throne, it will be her duty to convert all to Roman Catholicism. Grigory—now called Dmitri—arrives, and Marina's seduction is complete.

In Act IV, the opposing forces draw closer to the throne; a revolution is fomenting. Back at the Kremlin, Shuisky introduces Pimen, who tells a story about a miracle at the grave of the former tsarevich. Boris, now haunted by the evils of his past, is overwhelmed and realizes that he is dying. He passes his rule to his son and then dies, begging for God's forgiveness.

BOZHE MOI! MOMENTS

Prologue: Boris's coronation scene: the people demand that Boris become tsar; he accepts with a heavy heart as a remarkable cacophony of bells toll.

Act I: Pimen's cell: This is a gloomy scene but one which explains the entire plot. It also has a mystical and religious aura about it that clarifies a great many of the people's beliefs: dreams, omens, etc. In Scene ii, in the inn, Varlaam sings a wild—and wildly entertaining—song about his life as a soldier in the army of Ivan the Terrible. It does not help the plot, but it's a spectacular showpiece for a big-voiced bass and a momentary diversion from the gloom.

Act II: The clock scene: After a fine scene for Boris and his children in which he confesses his anguish and remorse to his son, the double-dealing Shuisky tells Boris of the rise of a pretender in Poland and torments the tsar with a story of how, a full five days after the tsarevich's murder, the body still had not putrified and there was a smile on his face. Boris, practically suffocating, breaks down and, watching a chiming clock with moving figures, believes he is seeing the murdered child. Certainly one of the greatest scenes for bass voice in all of opera.

Act III: Both Marina's aria and the duet for Marina and the pretender are handsome pieces of music—passionately composed, filled with melodic inspiration. But they are unnecessary to the plot.

Act IV: In the Council Hall of the Kremlin—Pimen's monologue and Boris's death scene. Simply the icing on the cake: we watch a once powerful man fall apart and die, driven insane by his own guilt.

Pyotr Ilyich Tchaikovsky

Pyotr Ilyich Tchaikovsky (1840–1893) is famous to non–music lovers for a single piece. Yes, every teeny ballerina's holiday fave, *The Nutcracker* (can you imagine how much the residuals on it would be if it weren't in the public domain?). Amid all the sugar-plums and dancing mice and snowflakes, it's almost too easy to forget how brilliant a composer Tchaikovsky actually was; there are many great musical reasons his work is still so performed and beloved. Non–opera lovers barely know that he composed operas—they concentrate on the symphonies and piano concerti, which are as famous as they are popular.

Born in deepest Russia (in Votkinsk in the province of Vyatka), the young Pyotr Ilyich showed musical promise early on—much to the consternation of his rather bureaucratically inclined middle-class family. Hoping to prepare their son for a useful career, his parents sent him off to the School of Jurisprudence in St. Petersburg. After the proverbial college try, he took a job at the Ministry of Justice. Perhaps that would have been it, but he began attending classes at the St. Petersburg Conservatory and soon enough quit public service. His success was almost immediate. His most famous operas today are *Eugene Onegin* and *The Queen of Spades* (*Pikovaya Dama*).

Though Tchaikovsky was famous and popular through much of his life, he was also neurotic and miserable. Early in his career, while conducting, he got the impression that his head was about to fall off, and he led the rest of the performance with one hand supporting it. (This is not a joke.) Perhaps this was a result of his homosexuality, which he hid with great determination; perhaps early childhood traumas never worked themselves out; or maybe he was simply a sadly tortured genius. It's hard not to wish that the composer had come of age in a time and place more suited to his sexual orientation and delicacy of spirit.

Eugene Onegin

Three acts

First professional performance: Bolshoi Theater, Moscow, 1881

Libretto: Written by the composer with Konstantin Shilovsky, after Pushkin's poem of the same name

In *Eugene Onegin*, the disdainful and vain title character spurns the love offered by the young and dreamy Tatiana. Much later, when she has blossomed into a beautiful woman, he changes his mind and pursues her. However, his brashness has caused too much grief in the intervening years, and he is doomed to live alone with his past mistakes.

While Tchaikovsky was at work on *Eugene Onegin*, a young student named Antonina Miliukova was courting him; indeed, she was begging him to marry her. Though already famous, Tchaikovsky was anxious about everything from his career to his (to him) shameful and perplexing homosexuality, and he certainly did not want to wind up like Onegin. So, with catastrophic results, he gave in to Antonina's pressure. He fled his wife almost at once, following up the abandonment with a nervous breakdown and a suicide attempt. Antonina pleaded and threatened blackmail for years; she was finally committed to an insane asylum, where she spent the rest of her life—yet another example of life being more operatic than opera.

WHO'S WHO

Tatiana, a young girl (soprano)
Olga, Tatiana's sister (mezzo-soprano)
Vladimir Lensky, Olga's suitor (tenor)
Eugene Onegin, Vladimir's friend (baritone)
Prince Gremin (bass)

WHAT'S HAPPENING

The Russian countryside and St. Petersburg, late eighteenth century

In Act I, left in the background by her sister Olga's engagement to Lensky, Tatiana falls for and declares her love to Lensky's friend Onegin in a flowery letter. At their next meeting, he chides her for her impetuous behavior.

Act II brings a gala ball given by Olga and Tatiana's mother. Onegin shows up in bad temper and spends the time flirting with Olga. Lensky objects, the two friends duel, and after the pistols have been fired, Lensky is dead.

Act III begins three years later, in St. Petersburg. Onegin attends another ball, but without any joy; his conscience and cynicism have dogged his days, although he is only twenty-six. Prince

Gremin introduces his lovely wife, Tatiana. Onegin feels a sudden rush of passion for her, as well as hope for a new and better life. When they are alone together, she admits she still loves him but now has the control over her emotions he once admonished her for lacking. She will never give in, and he is left to despair.

BOZHE MOI! MOMENTS

Act I: Tatiana's letter scene, "Puskai pogibnu ya," a lengthy confession of love that takes the impressionable girl through many moods (and tempi). A quick expression of feeling alive is followed by an introspective, sweet plea to Onegin that he not humiliate her; this is backed by a plaintive oboe. Finally she writes, "I am alone here. I will trust all to you." Knowing the outcome, this is heartbreaking. In the next, brief scene they meet again, and he tells her to use self-control: "Not everyone will be as nice as I" (the duet "Zdyes on, zdyes on, Yevgeni!").

Act II: "Kuda, kuda, kuda vi udalilis" is an expression of grief from Lensky: What happened to my happy future? he asks; then he thinks of Olga and accepts his fate. The aria is like an oasis of pure emotion on a par with Tatiana's letter scene—a character laid bare.

Act III: Gremin's aria "Lyubvi vsye vozrasti pokorni" is a glorious moment for bass. He confesses that love came to him late but Tatiana has transformed his life. As in Tatiana's and Lensky's arias, we get great insights (and beautiful melodies and orchestrations) in just a few minutes. And Onegin and Tatiana's final duet, "O! Kak mnye tyazhelo!," is a heart-ripping series of confessions and admissions that leave Onegin emotionally shattered.

Epilogue

AND FINALLY . . .

Well, there you have fifty operas to wrap your heads around. I can think of another fifty that are just as or more crucial, that will give as much or more pleasure. The "standard" repertoire, that is to say, operas that are put on frequently in many houses around the world, probably comprises these fifty and another fifty; there are another two hundred that pop up occasionally and are worth knowing. Just to get us to 1850, and sticking only with truly great works, there are two more by Monteverdi, a big handful by Handel, a couple by Vivaldi, three more by Bellini, ten by Rossini and Donizetti, and four or five pre-*Rigoletto* works by Verdi, works from his early period. But with any luck, not only is opera now in enough perspective for you, but you know the type of thing to listen for so that you can explore by yourself. At any rate, just recognizing opera's magnificence and absurdities and approaching it with less angst or diffidence will guide you well.

I mentioned earlier in the book that if, in fact, opera is dying, it has been doing so for four hundred years. The common argument is that people who go to the opera are a bunch of gray heads; that the average age is, well, nearly dead. I recall this argument from the 1970s as well, when arts commentators were asking how younger people could be attracted to the opera. Why hasn't it dawned on everyone that (1) each year there's a new batch of gray heads, (2) perhaps opera is something that requires a certain degree of understanding and maturity, and (3) people in their thirties and forties are probably raising children and are either financially strapped or at home with the aforementioned children? The target age for most entertainment nowadays is eighteen to thirty; people of that age group are the ones with time and disposable income; they don't own homes, and they don't have kids. And they're really good at partying and drinking—why should they sit still for three hours with an art form that is alien to them? Leave them alone—they'll see an ad at their local movie house for an opera, and somehow the spark will be lit. Or wait until they're gray—it's only a few years down the line.

Furthermore, an article in *Time* online in May 2010 mentioned that the median age of operagoers is forty-eight. That isn't exactly geriatric; everyone knows someone who is actually forty-eight and still alert. In context, it was an article about opera in high definition and how it is helping reduce the age of the audience; this has been one of my arguments all along. Superb seats in the opera house can be obscenely expensive, and opera in the movie theaters has leveled that playing field. They are two different experiences, of course, and the cinema experience will certainly appeal more to those brought up on television, where close-ups rule, than on those of another era, who used to go to the theater and are accustomed to—and not bothered by—performers being hundreds of feet away. Most people at rock concerts are miles away from the stage as well, but huge TV screens and great sound systems bring them closer; very few people prefer binoculars over the reality of a natural, detailed view. But even some of my die-hard opera pals are finding they prefer the cinema experience; they like seeing the singers sweat.

There are valid arguments for both, but one thing about the experience of hearing opera singers in the flesh remains immutable: since opera houses do not use amplification of any kind, there is a primeval thrill at the sheer sound of the voice and its ability to be heard, in all its glory, from the quietest whisper to the grandest roar, sometimes from the equivalent of a fifth-floor window. And when you hear a soprano or tenor voice riding over an entire orchestra and chorus, it goes right through you, it leaves you agog; you appreciate the craft, the work, the dedication, much as you would a superbly executed alley-oop in basketball. It's a feat. Almost superhuman. Magic. Doesn't seem possible. And that's the last time I'll ever use a sports metaphor.

One last thought: as long as there are people who love music, hysterical fantasies of murder, dominance, envy, obsessive love or lust, inexplicable moments of rapture, expressions of rage, and emotional rebirth or destruction, there will always be reasons to listen to the opera. London's Royal Opera House is soon to release a performance of Bizet's *Carmen* in 3D. So technologically cool!

Index